EAT REAL Vietnamese FOOD

LOTUS

Nguyễn Hoàng Liên

Many thanks to all those who helped me throughout this project by offering their talent, time, ideas and criticism. They know how much I owe them.

Special thanks to my husband Charlie for his enthusiasm, love and support.

Published by Golden Lotus Publishing
Palo Alto, CA
Copyright © 2017 Lien Nguyen
All rights reserved.

Cover design and illustration by
CamilleMaiIllustration.com

Printed in the United States of America
First Printing 2017
ISBN print: 978-0-9862520-3-7
ISBN eBook: 978-0-9862520-4-4

www.EatRealFoodOrElse.com

Text and design - *Nguyễn Hoàng Liên*
Recipes - *Ngô Thi Dàng*
Photos - *Nguyễn Đạt Nhiếp, Nguyễn Hoàng Liên*
Photos pages 3, 8, 12, 14, 54, 74, 82, 86, 88, 96, 97, 106, 108, 112, 120, 141, 146, 150, 158, 166, 172, 174, 184, 192, 194, 200, 202, 209, 210, 240, 251, 255 - *Thịnh Lê*
Photos pages 62, 72, 74, 112 - *A.C. Lê Văn Đức*

By the same author:

Eat Real Food or Else
(Golden Lotus Publishing, 2016)
ISBN: 978-0-9862520-1-3

La cuisine Vietnamienne par l'image
(Editions Orphie, 2011)
ISBN: 978-2877636049

Le Haut Val d'Arly pas à pas
(Editions Orphie, 2012)
ISBN: 978-2877638449

CONTENTS

Preface

This book started as a quiet, innocuous enough project: a few years ago, I decided to learn more about Vietnamese cooking, because, after all, it is my cultural heritage, and also because I love to eat! My mother had a collection of recipes, some neatly gathered in a notebook, but most scribbled on loose sheets of paper, often presenting several conflicting versions of the same dish. So, I decided to sort it out and write down what she thought was the best version for each of her specialties.

Any undertaking of mine has a tendency toward "mission creep," as my husband will tell you, and this one was no exception. As I was moving along, this gradually became a project to immortalize a disappearing way of life. We decided to focus on my mom's domain of expertise: Vietnamese food from the early 50s.

Vietnam has a long, restless history, and the 20th century was particularly rich in turmoils. These difficult, troubled times make the 50s particularly interesting in the culinary sense: in those years, many Vietnamese people emigrated from the North (including my father's family) and settled in the South, bringing with them, among other things, different ways of cooking and eating. They didn't always have access to authentic Southern cuisine: old classics were modified, sometimes happily reinterpreted, sometimes badly misunderstood. Later in the century, more changes followed with the American presence, and some more with the new affluence of peacetime.

This book's ambition is to be a time capsule from the middle of last century, when South Vietnamese cuisine was still influenced by French culture, and before it evolved radically with the arrival of immigrants from the North.

I might be partial, but I feel that the cuisine of that time is particularly refined and worthy of being preserved. It is part of my parents' cultural legacy and, to me, it is the classic cuisine of Vietnam.

Nguyễn Hoàng Liên
Palo Alto, February 2017

To my parents
For my children

An asterisk refers to another recipe in this book (see "Table of Contents" on page 252).

All the ingredients are presented in detail in the appendix at the end of the book (see "Index and Glossary" on page 241).

The little hourglass icons above the list of ingredients provide an indication of the complexity of the recipe, not an exact cooking time!

All the quantities have been specified with care. However, remember that it is the privilege and the duty of cooks to adjust the seasoning to their taste. Perfection is sometimes only a matter of balance...

Starters
and Small Plates

Pâtés Chauds
Ba Tê Sô

This delicious little meat pie is an adaptation of the French *pâté en croûte,* from which it inherited its name. In spite of its popular origins, it is enjoyed by Vietnamese people from all walks of life. It is sold in the streets from small glass-paned carts to the shouts of *"Ba tê sô!".* It can eaten at any time of day, but is especially appreciated for breakfast.

For 48 pâtés ~ ⧖ ⧖ ⧖

- 1 large onion
- 1 lb ground pork (lean shoulder)
- 3 tablespoons pure fish sauce (*nước mắm*)
- ½ teaspoon pepper
- 1½ lb puff pastry
- 1 egg

Seasoning with *nước mắm* is my mom's innovation: normally, only salt is used, but the fish sauce makes the stuffing much tastier. An ideal dish for a snack or a picnic, it is popular with young and old alike.

1. Using a rolling pin, roll out the puff pastry as needed to get sheets about ¹⁄₁₀ of an inch thick. Cut it into circles about 4 inches in diameter.

2. Dice the onion by hand very finely. Mix in all the other ingredients except for the egg. Beat the egg yolk together with a spoonful of water.

3. Baste the inside edge of each pastry circle with beaten egg yolk, fill with a heaping teaspoon of stuffing, and close. Pinch well to seal around the edges, making a wide enough border so that the pie doesn't come apart while cooking.

4. Preheat the oven to 390 °F. Place the little pies on a baking sheet lined with parchment paper. Baste the top of each pie with some beaten egg yolk.

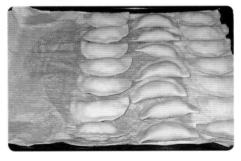

Cook for about 15 minutes. The exact time may vary depending on the type of puff pastry and the size of the pies.

REMARKS

The little pies can be round or, more elegantly, shaped as half moons.

Frozen puff pastry is difficult to deal with, as it softens too much and has a tendency to become sticky when handled.

Steamed Pork Buns
Bánh Bao

For 16 buns ~
⧖ ⧖ ⧖ ⧖

Dough:

- 1 cup whole milk
- 3 cups steamed bun flour mix (*bột bánh bao*)
- ½ cup granulated sugar

Stuffing:

- 1 lb ground pork (rib or shoulder), not too lean
- 2 tablespoons oyster sauce (*dầu hào*)
- 1 tablespoon granulated sugar
- 8 hard-boiled eggs, peeled and cut in half
- 4 Chinese sausages (*lạp xưởng*), sliced ⅛-inch thick
- 8 dry shiitake mushrooms (*nấm hương*), soaked overnight, then drained and cut in half

Bánh bao with a ground pork filling is a popular street food. It is bigger and less refined than *bánh bao* with roast pork. All the ingredients are Chinese; therefore, *nước mắm* is absent. However, unlike the Chinese, Vietnamese people use milk to make the dough: this yields a smoother, richer bun.

In some places, *bánh bao* is considered a success only if the dough, once cooked, is smooth and almost white with a very thin skin that can be peeled off. It is safer to buy an especially formulated flour mix; regular wheat flour often results in a chewy dough that is not soft enough to the tooth.

1. Thoroughly dissolve the sugar in the milk. Add the flour and knead for about 10 minutes. (These instructions and proportions are approximate; follow the flour manufacturer's instructions.) After powdering your hands with flour, roll the dough into balls slightly smaller than a ping-pong ball (1¼ oz).

2. Prepare the ingredients for the stuffing. Avoid cutting the sausage diagonally as the pointy corners may poke through the dough wrapping. Season the pork with the oyster sauce and sugar.

3. Flatten one ball of dough with a rolling pin. The secret of success is to make it not too thin, about 4 inches in diameter.

4. On the dough circle, place a tablespoon of pork, then an egg half and some Chinese sausage. Top with a piece of mushroom.

5. Wrap the dough around the filling by pulling and gathering the edges little by little. The dough should show a few creases at the top. Pinch firmly shut, so the bun doesn't open up while cooking.

Let the dough rise for 10 minutes. Cook the buns in a steamer for 15 minutes. Just before serving, steam again to reheat.

REMARKS

If the sugar isn't fully dissolved, the outside of the bun will be pockmarked rather than smooth. On the other hand, there is no need to knead the dough for longer than 10 minutes, as it may become rubbery. It is preferable to let the dough sit *after* making it into balls rather than before.

Beware! Some brands of oyster sauce are very salty, others less so. Taste and adjust the amount of seasoning accordingly.

Bánh bao xá xíu: buy roast pork from a Chinese deli. Slice into thin strips, taking care to avoid pointy corners. Add a little of the roasted meat sauce and use this for the stuffing.

Meat and Mushroom Dumplings
Bánh Giò

In Vietnam of old, this pyramid-shaped dumpling wrapped in banana leaves was sold only by street vendors, never in restaurants. The ball of meat in its core was really tiny...

Nowadays, the contrast between "rich" and "poor" foods has faded, and this dish is beloved by all. Its newly acquired distinction allows it to appear on the family dining table, though still not in restaurants. It is presented here as an appetizer, but in Vietnam it would be eaten at any time, particularly for breakfast or as an afternoon snack.

This unpretentious dumpling is nevertheless time-consuming and tricky to prepare. The batter is quite easily botched, and it is of the utmost importance to respect the exact quantities and temperatures specified in this recipe. The batter was traditionally prepared with rice flour, but here we will use flours closer to current tastes. Also, in place of the banana leaf, we will wrap the dumplings with the somewhat less traditional, but more practical, aluminum foil.

For 35 dumplings ~ ⧗ ⧗ ⧗ ⧗

Stuffing:
- 1½ lb ground pork (shoulder, not too lean)
- 3 oz wood ear mushrooms (nấm mèo)
- 3 large onions
- 8 tablespoons pure fish sauce (nước mắm)
- 1 heaping tablespoon pepper

Batter:
- 500 g cornstarch
- 250 g potato starch
- 1 heaping tablespoon salt
- 1 tablespoon mushroom seasoning (optional)
- 1 litre (exactly) warm water at 100 °F (38 °C)
- 1.6 litre (exactly) boiling water at 212 °F (100 °C)

1. Preparation of the stuffing

Soak the dry mushrooms for 1 to 2 hours. Drain and chop into small bits using a knife. Don't forget to remove the hard center part; otherwise, the dumplings will be impossible to eat.

Dice the onions very finely using a sharp knife so that they remain crisp.

Combine all the stuffing ingredients.

2. Preparation of the batter

In a large pan, mix the two flours, the salt, and the mushroom seasoning. Add the warm water (100 °F) and stir rapidly: at this temperature, the flour will not become lumpy. Then pour in the boiling water slowly while stirring the mix with a spatula. Keep on stirring while the flour "sets" until the batter is soft and smooth (less than a minute). It should acquire the consistency of a soft purée, and should not fall from the spoon.

In case this doesn't work (wrong water temperature), heat the pan gently, while continuously stirring the batter until it sets, about 15 minutes. Be sure to scrape off the bottom thoroughly in order to avoid lumps, which would render the batter useless.

Wait 15 minutes for the batter to cool off before using. However, as making the dumplings with cold batter is quite difficult, it's better if two people work together to speed up the fabrication process while the batter is exactly at the right temperature.

3. Forming the dumplings

Cut the aluminum foil into 8 x 16-inch rectangles. Brush some oil on the center of each piece.

Place a heaping tablespoon of batter in the center without spreading it.

Add some stuffing, roughly the size of a ping pong ball.

On top of this, add another half tablespoon of batter.

Using a knife, close the dumpling by bringing the side edges of the batter up toward the top. Smooth the surface rapidly.

Close up the aluminum foil by bringing two sides together and folding several times.

Then close the sides that are still open by folding the foil underneath. The result should be roughly cubical, about 2 inches wide, somewhat narrower at the top.

4. Cooking

Bring a large pot of water to a boil, adding a full tablespoon of vinegar to prevent the aluminum foil from darkening. Boil the dumplings for 20 minutes.

Remove the aluminum foil only before serving. You'll need to wait half an hour to an hour after cooking; otherwise, the soft dough will stick to the foil. If you prepared the dumplings ahead of time, reheat them in their aluminum foil in boiling water for 5 minutes, after which you can discard the foil and serve immediately.

Serve warm. Each guest adds a bit of pepper and pure fish sauce according to their taste.

REMARKS

Use freshly ground white pepper. The amount of fish sauce specified may seem excessive, but in order to taste good, the dough needs to absorb some of it. The mushroom powder, although optional, is the secret of a tasty dough...

The water temperatures are very important. The boiling water must have been boiling right before it is poured. It's a lot more trouble if the batter needs to be thickened some more later.

For the ultimate refinement, place a banana leaf on the aluminum foil before making the dumplings. This way the batter will absorb some of the banana leaf flavor. However, beware: forming the dumplings becomes harder. Soak the banana leaves in boiling water beforehand to soften them.

Shrimp and Sweet Potato Fritters
Bánh Tôm

This dish appeals to all Vietnamese people, from North to South. In the past, it was considered common street food and would never be served in a nice home, only on street corners. In the North, *bánh tôm Hồ Tây,* fried to perfection, its dough thin and crispy, was especially renowned.

Since 1975, Vietnamese immigrants have introduced many of these modest but beloved dishes into restaurants abroad. This practice has also spread in Vietnam, where very fancy fritters with scalloped edges can sometimes be found in restaurants. White potatoes produce crispier fritters, but sweet potato has the advantage of being, well, slightly sweet.

For 16 small fritters ~ ⧗ ⧗

- 32 medium-sized shrimp, shell-on, with very thin shells
- 1 sweet potato (*khoai lang*) or 2 large white potatoes
- 1 cup wheat flour
- 1 tablespoon potato starch
- 1 teaspoon baking powder
- 1 pinch of salt
- Water
- Oil for frying

1. Wash the shrimp. Using scissors, cut off the legs and the tips of the heads up to the eyes. You can also discard the entire head if you wish. Dry well.

2. Peel the sweet potato and cut it into very thin matchsticks, about 1/16 inch across. Rinse in cold water to eliminate the excess starch. Wipe dry very carefully.

3. Mix the flour, starch, baking powder, and salt. Add water gradually while stirring with a spoon or electric mixer, until you get a fairly liquid batter that flows without breaking apart. Let sit for 30 minutes.

4. Using a small flat ladle, scoop a small amount of batter, spread a layer of sweet potato strips on it, and top with two shrimp. Dip it in boiling oil and, after the batter has set, remove the ladle. Shape the fritter into a disk about 2 inches across. Turn it over to brown the other side. Drain.

Sprinkle with salt and serve piping hot, as an appetizer. You can also eat these like Imperial Rolls*, that is, accompanied by an Aromatic Herb Platter* and *Nước Mắm* Dip* (skip the salt seasoning in this case).

REMARKS

The shrimp should be about the size of a little finger, and the shells very thin so they don't scratch the throat... Vietnamese people love to eat the heads, but watch out: if they come off during frying, the yellow stuff inside ruins everything.

If you use regular potatoes, select a type that is fairly firm and not too starchy. In Vietnam, regular potatoes are expensive and only sweet potatoes are used.

Before making the first fritter, preheat the ladle by dipping it into the hot oil; otherwise, the batter will stick to the metal. You can also make the fritters by pouring the batter directly into the oil and shaping the fritters in the pan.

Sizzling Crêpes

Bánh Xèo

These crispy treats are delicious when they are sizzling hot, straight out of the frying pan. Although many recipes call for a profusion of ingredients, we favor simplicity. *Bánh xèo* is best when the dough is very crispy on the outside, the inside remaining soft and moist.

In Central Vietnam, *bánh khoái* is similar, a bit smaller, but it is served with peanut sauce instead. Those who can't afford several crêpes eat a single one with a heap of herbs. As a main course, figure one crêpe per person; as an appetizer, one crêpe for two.

Bánh xèo is accompanied by *nước mắm* dip and a large aromatic herb platter.

For 8 crêpes ~ ⧗⧗

- 1 bag (14 oz) *bánh xèo* flour mix (*bột bánh xèo*)
- 1 onion
- 6 oz raw pork shoulder
- 8 oz medium shelled shrimp
- 8 oz mung bean sprouts (*giá*)
- ⅓ cup mung beans (*đậu xanh*), optional
- Peanut oil

Serve with:

- Aromatic Herb Platter (*Diã Rau Sống*)*
- *Nước Mắm* Dip (*Nước Mắm Pha*)*

1. Prepare the batter according to the manufacturer's instructions: it should run as a continuous ribbon, a little thinner than regular crêpe batter. Let it sit for at least 1 hour.

2. Meanwhile, prepare the garnish:
   - Slice the onion.
   - Cut the meat into slices approximately ½ x 1 x ⅛ inches.
   - Wash and dry the shrimp.
   - Wash and drain the bean sprouts.

3. If necessary, make bean paste (the beans should have been soaking overnight): drain the beans, place in a pot with enough water to cover, bring to a boil, and then lower the heat as much as possible. Turn off the heat after 5 or 10 minutes and crush with a spoon to obtain a thick paste.

4. In a medium-sized (8 or 9 inches in diameter) nonstick skillet, pour a good layer of oil (about ⅛-inch thick) and heat on very high heat.

5. When the oil is very hot, place 2 or 3 pieces of meat and a few slices of onion in the skillet. Let them cook a few seconds. Mix the batter well and pour a ladleful on top of the meat and onions. Spread the batter in the skillet as if making a regular crêpe.

6. On top of the batter, place several shrimp, a small handful of sprouts, and optionally a teaspoon of bean paste.

7. Cover and let cook about 10 minutes. Periodically check that it is not burning: lower the heat after a few minutes if necessary.

Fold the crêpe in half and slide onto a platter. Serve immediately with *Nước Mắm* Dip* and a large Aromatic Herb Platter*. Each person breaks off a piece of crêpe, wraps it in a salad leaf, and dips it in an individual bowl of dipping sauce before eating.

REMARK

The crêpes must be cooked as the guests eat them, since *bánh xèo* must be eaten very hot! Because of this, it's better for the guests to share large crêpes from a common platter rather than having individual ones.

Fresh Rolls

Bò Cuốn, Bì Cuốn, Nem Cuốn

Here are some delicious rolls that present tasty alternatives to the ubiquitous spring roll. They are all prepared in the same manner. Only the meat garnish varies. They can be served as an appetizer along with spring rolls; however, these fresh rolls are dipped into *nước mắm* rather than peanut sauce.

Outside Vietnam, mint leaves prevail, as they are readily available, but in Vietnam, mint is not particularly special, and all kinds of other aromatic leaves are used.

For 12 rolls ~ ⌛ ⌛ ⌛

- 12 rice paper sheets (*bánh tráng*), 8 inches in diameter
- ½ lettuce or other large salad leaves
- Herbs: mint, polygonum (*rau răm*), perilla (*tía tô*), etc.

Meat, either:

- 1 lb Shredded Pork (*Bì*)*
- 1 lb Sautéed Beef with Lemongrass (*Bò Xào Sả*)*
- 12 small fermented pâtés (*nem chua*)

Dipping:

- 1 cup *Nước Mắm* Dip (*Nước Mắm Pha*)*

1. Wash the herbs and salad leaves. The rolling will be easier if the hard center of the lettuce leaves is removed.

2. If you use fermented pork pâtés, cut each piece in half, crush and stretch into two little cylinders 4 to 5 inches long.

3. Quickly dip a sheet of rice paper in water, and then lay it on a dry kitchen towel. Wait 1 or 2 minutes for it to become pliable. On top, place a piece of lettuce leaf, some herbs, and the meat, either:
   - A bit of shredded pork
   - 1 fermented pork pâté cylinder
   - Or some sautéed beef

4. Fold the two sides over and then roll up. To get a good-looking roll, you must press tightly, but not so tight as to tear the rice paper (use all your fingers!). Repeat for all the rolls. Replace the towel when it becomes too wet.

A bowl of bì

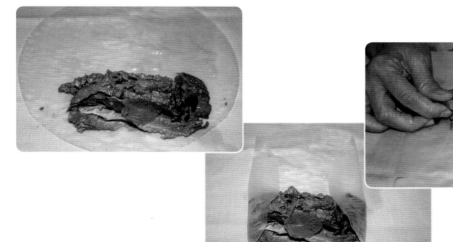

Cover the plate of finished rolls with a damp cloth to prevent the rice paper from drying and hardening. Serve as an appetizer; provide *Nước Mắm* Dip* in small individual dipping bowls and chili pepper.

REMARKS

Don't soak the rice paper for too long. Pass it rapidly through the water and let it sit 1-2 minutes.

You can buy ready-made shredded pork or prepare it yourself.

For a family meal, serve the entire rolls. For a more elegant alternative, discard the ends (which are just wadded folds of rice paper), and cut the remaining rolls into 1-inch-long pieces.

Fried Fish Cake
Chả Cá Thác Lác

Serves 4 ~ ⧗

- 8 oz frozen notopterus (*cá thác lác*)
- 5 sprigs Vietnamese dill (*thìa là*)
- 1½ tablespoons pure fish sauce (*nước mắm*)
- ¼ teaspoon white pepper
- Peanut oil

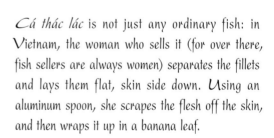

Cá thác lác is not just any ordinary fish: in Vietnam, the woman who sells it (for over there, fish sellers are always women) separates the fillets and lays them flat, skin side down. Using an aluminum spoon, she scrapes the flesh off the skin, and then wraps it up in a banana leaf.

You can use it to make soup (*Canh Cá Thác Lác**) or, as shown here, a delicious fish cake with only a few ingredients and very little effort.

1. Leave the fish to thaw overnight in the refrigerator (and not in warm water).

2. Wash the Vietnamese dill. Chop it into large pieces, discarding the hard ends of the stalks.

3. In a large bowl, combine the fish, chopped dill, fish sauce, and pepper. "Knead" using a large metal spoon: scrape and press the surface of the mix as if to smooth it, until you get a homogeneous and elastic paste (about 10 minutes).

4. Cover the paste in plastic wrap to prevent sticking, and, using a rolling pin, shape it into a pancake about ¾-inch thick.

5. Pour a thick layer (about ¼-inch deep) of oil into a skillet. Heat it over medium heat. Slide the pancake in and let it cook for 5 minutes on each side. The outside should turn golden and the inside should be fully cooked.

Cut the pancake into little squares and arrange them on a platter. You can serve it as an appetizer or as a main course with rice.

REMARK

We recommend you mix everything at the same time, because the fish paste becomes very firm once kneaded only a bit: at that point it becomes difficult to add in other ingredients.

Crab Pâté

Chả Cua

This dish can be found everywhere in Vietnam, but it is especially widespread in the South, where crab is abundant. Around *Nha Trang* or *Huế, chả cua* is prepared with the succulent *ghẹ;* further south, *ghẹ* disappears and is replaced by a blue crab that resembles Dungeness crab. In fact, in the United States, you should use Dungeness crab, whose meat is closest to that of Vietnamese crab.

For 4 pâtés ~ 🥢🥢🥢🥢

- 1 oz mung bean thread (*miến*)
- 1 lb crabmeat
  (2 or 3 Dungeness crabs)
- 1 shallot
  or white parts of 4 scallions (*hành lá*)
- 3 large eggs
- ¼ teaspoon salt
- ¼ teaspoon pepper
- 1 teaspoon pure fish sauce
  (*nước mắm*)

The seasoning for this dish must be very delicate: don't go overboard with pepper or salt. The egg yolk and fish sauce mix gives the surface of the pâté its appealing orange hue.

1. Soak the bean thread in warm water for ½ hour. Dry them WELL, and then, using scissors, cut them into 2-inch-long strands.

2. Kill the crabs by piercing them in the middle with the tip of a knife. Wash them and cook them in a pot of boiling water for 15 minutes.

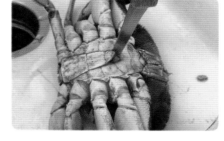

3. Shell the crabs completely, including the legs. Drain the meat very carefully: line a sieve with paper towels, put the meat on top, and press lightly on the surface using another paper towel.

4. Chop the shallots finely with a knife (never with a food processor: it would crush them). If you use scallions, slice them very thinly.

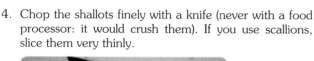

5. Combine the crabmeat, shallot, pepper, salt if necessary, the egg whites (set aside the yolks), and the bean thread.

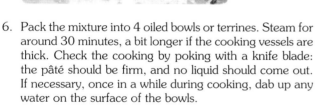

6. Pack the mixture into 4 oiled bowls or terrines. Steam for around 30 minutes, a bit longer if the cooking vessels are thick. Check the cooking by poking with a knife blade: the pâté should be firm, and no liquid should come out. If necessary, once in a while during cooking, dab up any water on the surface of the bowls.

7. Beat the egg yolks with the pure fish sauce. Baste a fairly thick layer onto the entire surface of each pâté and decorate with a few cilantro leaves. Steam again uncovered until the egg layer is cooked.

Serve in the cooking dish or unmold. Accompany with rice.

REMARKS

The quality of the crab is essential for the success of this dish. Above all, don't use low-quality canned crabmeat.

It is preferable to kill the crab before cooking: otherwise, they say, the legs will fall off during cooking and the meat will lose its juice.

Save this expensive and elegant dish for special occasions: *têt* or the anniversary of an ancestor. It is eaten in small amounts: figure one bowl of crab pâté for 4 people.

Imperial Rolls
Chả Giò

This national dish is also known as *"nem Sài-Gòn"* in North Vietnam (the word *nem* designating any food with a base of ground meat) or simply *"nem"* outside Vietnam. It is eaten on street corners as well as at the table on grand occasions. It is 100% Vietnamese, although many countries have adopted it with some variations. The use of rice paper remains, nevertheless, specifically Vietnamese.

The secret for preventing the roll from exploding? Avoid leaving pockets of air inside when rolling, and don't fry with too much heat.

For 60 small rolls ~ ⌛ ⌛ ⌛ ⌛

For the stuffing:

- 1½ lb ground pork shoulder, not too lean
- 14 oz crabmeat
- 2 oz mung bean thread (*miến*)
- 2 onions
- 2 carrots or 1 jicama (*củ sắn*)
- 1 scant tablespoon salt
- 1 teaspoon pepper

For the rolls:

- 60 rice paper sheets (*bánh tráng*), 7 inches in diameter

For serving:

- Aromatic Herb Platter (*Diã Rau Sống*)*
- *Nước Mắm* Dip (*Nước Mắm Pha*)*

1. Soak the mung bean thread, but not too long, just enough to be able to cut it in pieces (2 inches long). Keep it a bit dry so that it can absorb the juice from the stuffing.

2. Dice the onions into very small pieces, grate the carrot or jicama, shred the crabmeat. You can pour in the crab juice if there is not too much of it. Combine all the ingredients of the stuffing together.

3. Cover the workspace with a dry kitchen towel.

Quickly dip a sheet of rice paper in water, place it on the kitchen towel, wait 1 or 2 minutes for it to soften. Fold one edge.

Place on top a tablespoon of stuffing, spreading it so that the ends of the roll don't look too empty.

Fold the two sides, trying to gauge the width so that the rolls will end up identical: one way is to have the edges barely touch.

Roll, pressing fairly hard with all five fingers so that the roll is pretty, but not too tight, as the paper might tear.

4. Fry the rolls until golden brown, about 15 minutes, but watch that they don't burn!

If you intend to save them in the refrigerator or freezer, fry them only partially, until they are hard. You will fry them again just before serving.

Serve hot, accompanied with a heaping Aromatic Herb Platter* and *Nước Mắm* Dip*. Each guest takes a lettuce leaf, puts some herbs and a fried roll in it, rolls it up, and dips it in the fish sauce.

You can also serve this dish as an appetizer without accompaniment. In this case, it is better to make small rolls and spice up the stuffing with some pure fish sauce.

REMARKS

Don't soak the rice paper for too long: pass it rapidly through the water and let it sit 1 or 2 minutes before wrapping. Replace the kitchen towel if it gets too damp.

In South Vietnam, there is a sad tendency to abuse certain ingredients. Adding wood ear mushrooms (*nấm mèo*), soaked and then cut into small pieces, is optional. Carrots are not native to Vietnam; traditionally jicama is used instead.

Crispy Rice Salad

Cơm Cháy Nem Chua

This Laotian dish has recently been adopted by Vietnamese people. It was originally prepared with burnt rice from the bottom of the cooking pot. Now you can buy crispy rice cakes that are already seasoned in Vietnamese stores.

Be careful to mix in the rice only at the time of serving so that it will stay crunchy.

Serves 4 ~ ⧖

- 8 oz crispy rice (*Cơm cháy*)
- 3 sprigs cilantro (*ngò*)
- 3 sprigs culantro (*ngò gai*)
- 3 small fermented pâtés (*nem chua*)
- 1 tablespoon vinegar
- 1 level tablespoon granulated sugar
- 2 tablespoons water

1. Prepare the "sauce" by mixing well:
   - The vinegar
   - The sugar
   - The water

2. Finely chop the herbs along with their stems.

Ngò gai

3. Dice the pork pâtés into very small cubes.

Ngò

4. Let the herbs and meat marinate in the sauce for at least ½ hour.

A fried rice cake

5. Crumble the fried rice in a separate bowl.

Just before serving, combine everything together and transfer to the serving bowl.

REMARK

Fried rice used to be a hard-to-find commodity, but nowadays it is not rare to see it in Vietnamese food stores, either imported or made in-house.

Salty Fried Crab
Cua Rang Muối

Traditional
in the South,
this luxury dish is
costly, especially if the guests are hungry! As with
Crispy Salt Prawns (Tôm Rang Muối)*, in spite of
the dish's name *("muối"* means salt in Vietnamese), no salt
is used, since store-bought crab is already salty enough.

Figure one large crab per two people, which is
generous. Although Dungeness crab is quite good,
nothing equals the Vietnamese *ghẹ*!

Serves 6 ~ ⧗ ⧗ ⧗

- 3 Dungeness crabs
- ½ teaspoon pepper
- 1 small clove garlic
- 1 or 2 tablespoons wheat flour
- Peanut oil

1. Kill each crab by piercing it with the tip of a knife. Separate the hard outer shell by inserting the knife blade at the level of the crab's eyes and using it as a lever. Clean the crab by removing the brown and yellowish parts as well as the bladders.

2. Quarter each crab and slightly break the body and the legs with a hammer, but without mashing them entirely.

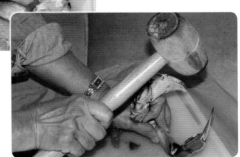

3. Season the crab with pepper and crushed garlic. Shake the container to mix well. Steam the crab rapidly (5 minutes), and then let it cool and air-dry.

4. Sprinkle all over with flour, including the pincers, making sure that any piece of flesh that sticks out is well coated. Distribute by shaking the container.

5. In a large frying pan, heat about ¼ inch of oil. Fry the crab over medium heat until the outside is just slightly browned, approximately 20 minutes.

REMARKS

You can reserve the shell and its contents to make a soup. Salt is necessary only with freshwater crabs. Be careful not to go overboard with the garlic!

You might be able to buy frozen Vietnamese crabs (ghẹ), which have the advantage of being easier to peel, as their shell is not so hard. (You can even crack it with your teeth!) Their taste is also more delicate.

Banana Blossom Salad
Gỏi Bắp Chuối

This uncommon, distinctive salad is the traditional accompaniment to Rice Porridge with Chicken (*Cháo Gà*)*: since making the broth for the porridge involves boiling a chicken, its meat is available for the salad.

An innovative refinement consists of replacing the chicken meat with duck breast.

Serves 6 ~ ⏳ ⏳ ⏳

- The meat from a boiled chicken
- 2 banana blossoms (*bắp chuối*)
- 1 small bunch polygonum (*rau răm*)
- 1 cup *Nước Mắm* Dip (*Nước Mắm Pha*)*
- ½ cup toasted peanuts
- Vinegar
- Salt

The banana "blossoms" are in fact the extremity of the banana bunch. They are sold fresh or canned in Asian supermarkets. The atrophied bananas that are found inside can sometimes be slightly bitter.

1. Soak the banana blossoms in a container of cold water with 2 added tablespoons of vinegar for 15 minutes. This will prevent them from turning dark when cooked.

2. Bring a pot of water to a boil and add another 2 tablespoons of vinegar with 1 teaspoon of salt. Place the banana blossoms in the boiling water and let them cook until they are tender: 30 minutes to 1 hour. Check the progress by poking them with a fork.

3. In the meantime, separate the chicken meat from the carcass and tear it into shreds by hand. Discard the skin, cartilage, fat, tendons, and in general anything that isn't pretty.

4. Open the blossoms and separate the small clusters of bananas; discard the larger ones if they are bitter. Discard the tough outer leaves. Cut the rest in half crosswise, then tear them into strips less than ½-inch wide. Possibly combine with some of the tiny bananas. Add 3 or 4 tablespoons of *Nước Mắm* Dip*, stir well, and let soak at least 30 minutes.

5. Drain the banana blossoms and press them to extract as much water as possible. Combine with the chopped herbs, chicken meat, and crushed peanuts.

Cooking these banana blossoms was not really a success as they turned brown instead of staying pink.

A cluster of little bananas

Place in front of each guest a bowl of Rice Porridge with Chicken*, a small plate of salad, and a small bowl of *Nước Mắm* Dip*. As an alternative, you can, of course, serve the salad on a common platter in the center.

REMARK

The fresh banana blossom oxidizes and turns gray upon contact with air. It is a good idea, therefore, to immerse it in a bowl of water with vinegar as soon as it is removed from its sealed package. Canned banana blossoms are much easier to use and yield good results.

Grapefruit Salad

Gỏi Bưởi

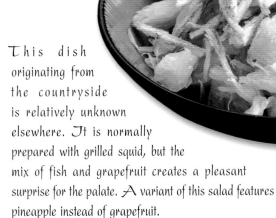

This dish originating from the countryside is relatively unknown elsewhere. It is normally prepared with grilled squid, but the mix of fish and grapefruit creates a pleasant surprise for the palate. A variant of this salad features pineapple instead of grapefruit.

If possible, use pomelo. This large Asian grapefruit is sweeter and easier to peel than regular grapefruit, owing to its thick inner skin. Make sure to add the shredded fish only at the last moment so it stays crunchy.

Serves 6 to 8 ~ ⧗ ⧗

- 1 Asian grapefruit (pomelo)
- 4 oz dried fish (*khô cá thiều*) or squid
- 1 cup *Nước Mắm* Dip (*Nước Mắm Pha*)*

1. Barely broil the dried fish: it is enough to put it in the microwave for 30 seconds or in a regular oven for 2 minutes. Watch out: it burns quickly! The fish should be brown, but not scorched and black.

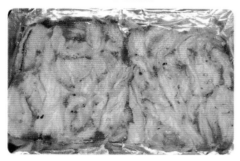

2. Shred the fish into thin pieces.

3. Peel the grapefruit. Remove the inner skin covering the sections. Crumble the flesh finely enough. Season with 4 or 5 tablespoons of *Nước Mắm* Dip*.

4. Just before serving, add the fish, mix and season to taste with *Nước Mắm* Dip*.

5. Arrange on a serving platter, and decorate with aromatic herbs. Like all the other *gỏi*, this salad is served with grilled rice paper (*bánh tráng*) or, alternatively, shrimp crackers (*bánh phồng tôm*).

Rice paper is prepared very quickly in the microwave.

REMARKS

Even though a pomelo seems small, it will yield more pulp than you may think...

You can replace the dried fish, which is sometimes hard to find, with dried squid, sold in all Asian markets.

It is important to properly season the fish sauce with garlic and chili pepper to bring out this dish's full flavor.

Spring Rolls
Gỏi Cuốn

These celebrated rolls can serve as a starter or simply be a snack. Out of negligence, some people will present them with diluted Hoisin sauce or worse still, *nước mắm* dip. However, the authentic accompaniment for this dish is peanut sauce.

For 12 rolls ~ ⧗ ⧗ ⧗

- 12 rice paper sheets (*bánh tráng*), 8 inches in diameter
- 7 oz fresh pork belly
- 1 lb medium-sized shrimp, 40/lb caliber
- 7 oz (½ package) rice noodles (*bún*)
- ½ lettuce or large salad leaves
- Fresh herbs: mint, polygonum (*rau răm*), perilla (*tía tô*), etc.
- 12 sprigs Chinese chive (*hẹ*)
- Mung bean sprouts (*giá*), optional

Sauce:

- 1 large bowl Peanut Sauce (*Tương Pha*)*

Dì Sáu is preparing a treat...

1. Cut the pork belly into slices ½-inch thick and cook in boiling water with a pinch of salt until tender (20 to 30 minutes). Discard the rind and cut the meat into slices 1/16-inch thick (or thinner if possible).

2. Cook, rinse, and carefully drain the Rice Noodles (Bún)*.

3. Rapidly cook the shrimp in boiling water (5 minutes). To economize, you can split them lengthwise, but keep in mind that they are tastier when they are kept whole.

4. Wash the herbs. Discard the hard central part of the lettuce leaves. Keep only 4 inches of the white end of the Chinese chives.

5. Briefly dip the rice paper in water and place it on a dry kitchen towel. Wait 1 or 2 minutes for it to soften. Place on top:
   - 3 shrimp
   - A salad leaf
   - Some aromatic herbs
   - A bit of noodles
   - A few pieces of meat
   - Optionally, bean sprouts

Fold the two sides. Place a sprig of Chinese chive on top, white end inside, so that the green head sticks out about 1 inch. Roll: you need to pull tight enough so that the roll looks tidy, but not so tight that the rice paper tears.

Serve as a starter along with little individual bowls of Peanut Sauce* for dipping.

REMARKS

You mustn't soak the rice paper too long: just pass it rapidly through the water and let it sit for 1 minute on the kitchen towel.

The shrimp do taste better if cooked in the shell, but are easier to peel and devein when raw. If shelled first, steaming is the preferred cooking method, as it's better at preserving the flavor.

You might be tempted to cook the pork belly without the rind in order to save time. However, the rind contributes some of the meat's flavor. It is preferable to cook a large piece of meat and cut it afterwards.

Avoid using the hard central part of the salad leaves, as the rolls will be hard to make. The commercially prepared rolls don't contain sprouts, because they tend to spoil rapidly.

Green Papaya Salad
Gỏi Đu Đủ Bò Khô

Unlike most others, this salad features Vietnamese basil *(rau húng quế)* instead of the usual polygonum *(rau răm),* and for once, peanuts are absent! You can decide to season it with either fish sauce or soy sauce.

Recently, it has become the style to serve it as an appetizer in the same fashion as the other *gỏi.* This was never done in the past: green papaya salad was mostly a treat you would buy on the street corner any time of day.

Serves 6 ~ ⏳

- 1 green papaya about 10 inches long *(đu đủ)*
- 1 cup *Nước Mắm* Dip *(Nước Mắm Pha)** or soy sauce dip
- 1 small bunch Vietnamese basil *(rau húng quế)*
- 4 oz dried beef slices *(khô bò)*

1. Peel the papaya, then grate with a small hand grater. Any other method would crush the flesh, causing it to lose its crunchiness. It is also a good idea to empty the fruit of its seeds before grating, as otherwise they may get mixed in with the rest.

This little grater is an indispensable tool.

2. Marinate the grated papaya in 6 tablespoons of *Nước Mắm* Dip*. You can replace the *Nước Mắm* Dip with a soy sauce dip that is prepared in the same fashion, substituting soy sauce for fish sauce. After a half hour, drain the water without pressing too hard so that the salad will retain some moisture.

3. Add the chopped herbs and mix. Season to taste with *Nước Mắm* Dip* or a soy sauce dip. Place on a serving platter.

4. Cut the dried beef into small strips (2 inches x ⅛ inch). Place them on top of the salad. Garnish with herbs and chili pepper.

REMARKS

Choose a nice fresh papaya. It need not be extremely green. Too large and the flesh will be rubbery; too young and it will be too soft. You need to pick a medium-sized fruit with taut skin.

This dish is eaten quite spicy. Sometimes fresh chili peppers are used, but more often bottled chili purée or chili sauce are the preferred condiment.

Remove the stalks before chopping the herbs with a knife! Keep a few pretty leaves for decoration.

You can prepare this plate ahead of time. It is one the easiest and fastest salads you can make!

Bamboo Shoot Salad
Gỏi Măng

Presented here is another traditional way to prepare *gỏi*, this time with bamboo shoots. In the South, it is sprinkled with crushed peanuts, whereas in the North sesame seeds are the norm.

Canned bamboo shoots are already cooked. The presence of striations inside is an indication that they will be tender. But watch out: you will need to rinse them many times to eliminate the smell. Sometimes you can find fresh bamboo (*măng mạnh tông*). Don't confuse these with the previously canned shoots sold in bulk; the fresh shoots are much better tasting and don't possess the unpleasant smell of the canned ones.

Serves 10 to 12 ~

- 2 cans of whole bamboo shoots (*măng*)
- 1 bunch polygonum (*rau răm*)
- ½ lb fresh pork belly
- ½ lb shrimp
- 2 tablespoons sesame seeds (*mè*) or ½ cup toasted and crushed peanuts
- 1 cup *Nước Mắm* Dip (*Nước Mắm Pha*)*

1. If using fresh shoots, cook them after discarding the hard part at their end. If canned, rinse well and dry.

2. Cut the shoots into match-sized sticks. Cut lengthwise, going with the grain, so they don't break. Add 5 or 6 tablespoons of *Nước Mắm Dip** and let sit for a half hour.

3. Chop the herbs.

4. Boil the pork in salted water until it is tender: 30 minutes to an hour (it goes faster if the meat is cut into slices around ½-inch thick). Remove the rind and cut the meat in slices ½ inch x 1/16 inch.

5. Cook the shrimp, devein and split them lengthwise (in that order).

6. Grill the sesame seeds over low heat, stirring continuously to avoid scorching them.

7. Combine the bamboo, meat and herbs, and then season to taste. Place on a platter, spreading the shrimp on top. Sprinkle with sesame seeds or crushed peanuts. Decorate with herbs and a chili pepper split lengthwise.

The ingredients, ready to be mixed at the last minute.

REMARKS

You can make this dish one hour or even a day in advance. It is easy, but takes relatively long to prepare.

The pork meat should be boiled long enough to become tender. For the shrimp, it is the opposite: plunge them into boiling salted water and pull them out as soon as they turn pink and opaque (2 minutes). If you don't, they will be about as tasty as cardboard...

Discard the stalks before chopping the herbs. Chop using a knife! Keep a few pretty leaves for the final decoration. If you have no polygonum, substitute another herb, mint for example.

Lotus Stem Salad

Gỏi Ngó Sen

This salad is the perfect example of a classical *gỏi*.

You can use fresh lotus stems or canned ones, which are usually already seasoned.

Serves 6 ~ ⏳ ⏳

- 7 oz shrimp
- 1 can (14 oz) lotus stems (*ngó sen*)
- ½ cucumber
- 1 stalk tender celery
- 1 carrot (optional)
- ½ cup peanuts, toasted and crushed
- 1 cup *Nước Mắm* Dip (*Nước Mắm Pha*)*
- 1 bunch polygonum (*rau răm*)

1. Shell and devein the shrimp, and cook them rapidly. Split them in two lengthwise (only after cooking).

2. Cut the vegetables:
   - Lotus stems: split lengthwise in 4
   - Cucumber: in slices or thin strips
   - Celery: diagonally in thin slices
   - Carrot: grated, for color

3. Marinate the vegetables in 5 or 6 tablespoons of *Nước Mắm* Dip*. After a half hour, drain well, pressing slightly to extract the water.

4. Add the chopped herbs, mix and season to taste with *Nước Mắm* Dip*.

5. Transfer to a serving platter. Sprinkle with crushed peanuts and place the shrimp on top. Decorate with herbs and a chili pepper split lengthwise.

REMARKS

Watch out: if the lotus stems are already seasoned, take that into account and use less fish sauce. In general, a 14 oz can of lotus stems will be largely sufficient. Even if they seem a bit meager, once taken out of the can and sliced, they do expand!

Discard the stems before chopping the herbs with a knife. Reserve a few pretty leaves for the garnish. Don't marinate the herbs: add them at the last minute so as to preserve their freshness.

You can prepare this dish in advance (a few hours or even a day). It is easy enough to make, but plan ahead, as it takes a while to prepare. However, it is always better to assemble the ingredients at the last moment.

pineapple Salad

Gỏi Thơm

Here is a dish in the same spirit as the *Grapefruit Salad (Gỏi Bưởi)**. It is typical of South Vietnam, which boasts an abundance of pineapple plantations. It is frequently eaten in the countryside.

You can select a pineapple that is more or less sweet, depending on your taste. Since pineapple is more tart than grapefruit, a little sauce is added in the fish, but be sure to mix it only at the last minute so the fish stays crunchy.

Serves 6 to 8 ~ ⧖ ⧖

- 1 pineapple
- 1 cucumber
- 1 bunch polygonum (*rau răm*)
- 3 oz dried fish (*khô cá thiều*) or dried squid
- 1 cup *Nước Mắm* Dip (*Nước Mắm Pha*)*

Sauce for the fish:

- 1 large crushed garlic clove
- 1 heaping teaspoon sugar
- 3 teaspoons vinegar or lemon
- 1 teaspoon chili purée

Serve with:

- Grilled thick rice paper (*bánh tráng*) or shrimp crackers (*bánh phòng tôm*)

1. Peel the pineapple, cut into eight sections, and remove the hard center. Cut each section into thin slices, ⅛-inch or thinner.

2. Peel the cucumber and split in two lengthwise. Remove the seedy core portion if needed. Slice very thinly (1/16-inch).

3. Combine the cucumber and pineapple with 6 to 8 tablespoons of *Nước Mắm* Dip*. Let sit for at least an hour.

4. Drain the excess water. Chop the polygonum very finely, then mix with the cucumber and pineapple. Season to taste with *Nước Mắm* Dip*. Place on a serving platter.

5. Roast the dried fish just enough to brown it (without burning it). You can simply cook it in the microwave for 30 seconds. Tear it into small strips by hand.

The fish here is slightly scorched: black spots are to be avoided.

6. Prepare a sauce by mixing the garlic, sugar, vinegar, and chili sauce.

Just before serving, mix the shredded dried fish and the sauce. Spread on top of the cucumber and pineapple on the serving dish. Decorate with herbs.

Like all the *gỏi,* this dish is served with thick grilled rice paper or, alternatively, shrimp crackers.

REMARKS

It is important to spice up the seasoning of the *Nước Mắm* Dip* with garlic and chili pepper.

Dried fish is difficult to find. Even if it is sold already cooked, it should be passed through the microwave oven as a hygienic measure, but watch out, it burns readily.

Green Papaya and Mango Salad
Gỏi Xoài Đu Đủ

**Serves
10 to 12** ~ ⧗ ⧗

- 1 green papaya (*đu đủ*)
- 1 green mango (*xoài*)
- 1 carrot (optional)
- ⅓ cup toasted peanuts
- ½ lb deveined cooked shrimp
- 1 small bunch polygonum
  (*rau răm*)
- 1 cup *Nước Mắm* Dip
  (*Nước Mắm Pha*)*

Gỏi is served with thick grilled rice paper sheets *(bánh tráng)* or, alternatively, shrimp crackers *(bánh phòng tôm).*

This salad is an adaptation of the very common green papaya and dried squid *gỏi*. Here we are adding mango to the traditional ingredients. Be sure to choose a mango that is very hard to the touch. The Kent species works well, being both crunchy and tart with a pleasant texture. As to the papaya, any kind will do as long as the fruit is the greenest possible.

1. Peel and grate the papaya, the mango, and optionally the carrot. For relative quantities, figure roughly equal amounts of papaya and mango. Other proportions are acceptable as well: *gỏi* is sometimes prepared using papaya only.

This little handheld grater is ideal for this purpose.

2. Marinate the grated papaya in 6 or 7 tablespoons of *Nước Mắm* Dip*. Drain after a half hour and press to remove some more water.

3. Combine with the grated mango and the chopped herbs. Mix and add (in moderation) some *Nước Mắm* Dip*.

Arrange on a serving platter, placing the shrimp on top. Sprinkle with crushed peanuts and decorate with a few herb leaves and a chili pepper split lengthwise. Guests should each have a small bowl of *Nước Mắm* Dip* so they can season their salad according to their taste.

REMARKS

When grating the papaya, be sure to avoid mixing seeds with the grated flesh!

Choose the greenest mango possible so that it will be crunchy. You can replace the mango with a large carrot or add just a few strings of grated carrot for color.

Don't marinate the mango or the herbs. Add them at the last minute so that they will stay crunchy.

Remove the stalks before chopping the herbs with a knife! Reserve a few pretty leaves for decoration.

The shrimp should be deveined and cooked. You can split them lengthwise (after cooking).

You can substitute other kinds of nuts for the peanuts, but watch out: they might be less crunchy. For aesthetic reasons, you can sprinkle the peanuts before placing the shrimp.

You can prepare this plate in advance (an hour or even a day). Though it is easy to make, reserve some time as it takes a while.

Crispy Salt Prawns
Tôm Rang Muối

In Vietnam, people will nibble on these shrimp while sipping alcohol *(nhậu)*. This dish can be served as an appetizer (not too convenient, as it is messy) or as a first course, but never as a main course with rice. The word *"rang"* refers to a cooking method that is halfway between frying and sautéing: more oil than for sautéing, but less than for frying.

It is best to use thin-shelled shrimp—for example, those from Madagascar. Paradoxically, although the name *"rang muối"* implies the use of salt *(muối)*, we do not add any here, as shrimp bought in the stores are already salty enough. In Vietnam, freshwater shrimp is the norm, hence the need for extra salt.

Serves 4 ~ ⧖

- 1 lb Asian prawns with the shell on, 15/lb caliber
- 1 tablespoon wheat flour
- Peanut oil

1. Cut off the shrimp's legs with scissors. An innovation: leave the head, just cutting the tip off, up to the eyes. When cooked, this will produce more juice, but it's good (if you like the head)! Otherwise, in general, the head is removed.

2. Wash the shrimp and dry them well. Powder them with flour, but not too much, we are not making fritters!

3. In a large pan, heat 4 or 5 generous tablespoons of oil over high heat. Add shrimp in a single layer. Stir rapidly. Remove them as soon as they are little crispy and lightly browned. Continue until all the shrimp are cooked, adding oil if necessary.

4. Drain on a paper towel, serve immediately.

REMARKS

For a family meal, you can save time by leaving the legs on; however, the dish is more elegant when they are removed.

If the shrimp are not dried well, the flour coating will be too thick.

Cook on maximum heat to prevent the shrimp from producing too much juice. The flour makes them crispy.

Main Courses

Angel Hair Prawns

Bánh Hỏi Tôm Nướng

Serves 6 ~ ⧖

- 12 large prawns (*tôm càng*) 8 inches long, or 6 small lobsters
- Rice vermicelli (angel hair, *bánh hỏi*), fresh or frozen
- 1 cup Scallion Oil (*Mỡ Hành Lá*)*
- ⅓ cup crushed toasted peanuts

Serve with:

- Aromatic Herb Platter (*Diã Rau Sống*)*
- *Nước Mắm* Dip (*Nước Mắm Pha*)*
- Fresh chili peppers

In the old days, this was just a simple dish that you could swallow quickly for breakfast at the market, squatting on the ground. It has now become quite expensive and fancy: for special occasions, the prawns can indeed be replaced by small lobsters. Crushed peanuts are not traditional here, but so tasty!

1. Brush the prawns with Scallion Oil*. If using lobsters, slice into the top of their shells and pour some Scallion Oil in there too.

2. Grill the prawns on high heat in an oven or on an electric grill (but not too long, otherwise, the prawns will lose their flavor).

Here, the prawn tails have been shelled before grilling.

3. Shell the prawns except for the head and the tip of the tail. Place on a serving platter and cover immediately with Scallion Oil* to prevent drying. Sprinkle some crushed peanuts on top.

Small lobsters

4. Steam the angel hair until it is soft. This happens quickly, even if the pasta was frozen. Garnish with Scallion Oil* before serving.

Angel hair in the steamer

The Angel Hair Prawns can be served "family style" on a common platter or on individual plates. In either case, accompany with *Nước Mắm* Dip*, a small plate of chili peppers, and a large Aromatic Herb Platter*.

REMARKS

This dish must be eaten with a lot of fresh greens, so don't hesitate to provide a mountain of aromatic herbs!

The *Nước Mắm* Dip* should be fairly diluted.

In Vietnam, the street vendors grill the entire prawn, and then they peel it before serving. For a meal at the table, it is perhaps more practical to shell the prawns before putting them in the oven. In any case, they should be thoroughly coated with Scallion Oil* to prevent drying.

Shredded Pork

Bì

The word "bì" means "skin" in Sino-Vietnamese, and in this dish, designates the pork rind. In Vietnam, the fresh rind is used, but this requires a long period of cleaning. Even though there is now ready-to-use rind, the preparation of this dish is labor-intensive. This is a bit paradoxical given it is absolutely not a luxury food.

For the meat, it's best to select pork fillet, which stays nice and almost white after cooking.

- 2 lb pork fillet
- 8 oz pork rind (*da bì*)
- 1 clove garlic
- ⅓ cup roasted rice flour (*thính*)
- Salt, pepper

Serve with:

- Mung bean sprouts (*giá*)
- Aromatic Herb Platter (*Dĩa Rau Sống*)*
- Rice Noodles (*Bún*)*
- Cucumber
- Scallion Oil (*Mỡ Hành Lá*)*
- Chili pepper (purée or fresh slices)
- *Nước Mắm* Dip (*Nước Mắm Pha*)*

1. Sprinkle the meat lightly with salt and pepper. Roast it in a medium oven for about 1 hour. Let it cool and harden.

2. Cut the fillet into ¹⁄₁₆-inch-thick slices. Then, stacking a few slices, cut again into strips about the thickness of kitchen matchsticks. Finally cut the "matchsticks" into 1-inch-long pieces. Cut all the meat in this manner.

3. Prepare the rind. If:
   - Fresh, already cut: sprinkle with a teaspoon of salt, knead lightly, fill the container with cold water, and rinse. Repeat 5 or 6 times. Above all, don't use warm water, or the rind will turn jellylike.
   - Frozen: defrost and rinse in the same way as above.
   - Dried: soak overnight. Then wash well, 15 times at least, until the rind loses its strong smell.

   In all cases, after rinsing, dry well with a kitchen towel and cut into 1-inch "matchsticks."

4. Combine the rind and meat, 2 parts meat to 1 part rind (by volume). Add the garlic, either finely chopped or crushed, the roasted rice flour, and a bit of salt. Mix, taste, and adjust seasoning accordingly.

Place in individual bowls, in this order:
- A dozen mung bean sprouts
- One lettuce leaf, filled with herbs, rolled and cut into ⅛-inch-thick slices
- A handful of cooked rice noodles

On top, place side by side, without mixing:
- The shredded pork
- A few slices of cucumber
- A tablespoon of Scallion Oil*
- A little bit of chili purée

Sprinkle on 1 or 2 tablespoons of *Nước Mắm* Dip*.

You can also serve Shredded Pork with rice, preferably "broken rice" (*cơm tấm*): each person puts some rice and pork in a bowl and seasons it copiously with spoonfuls of *Nước Mắm* Dip*. You can also roll Shredded Pork in rice paper (*Bì Cuốn*)*.

REMARKS

The work is greatly reduced if you own a meat-slicing machine. However, in any case, the last step of making the "matchsticks" must be completed by hand.

If you intend to freeze it, don't add the rice flour, as it will get wet and mushy. You can add it just before serving.

There are three types of pork rind (*da bì*):
- fresh: the best
- frozen: acceptable
- dried: our last choice, as it's yellow, has a strong odor, and takes a long time to wash.

For the meat, you can use pork loin as well, but fillet works better. Also, the loin is difficult to cut.

Grilled Beef and Rice Noodles
Bò Bún

Serves 8 ~ ⏳⏳

- 2 lb tender beef
- 2 stalks fresh lemongrass
- 1 teaspoon salt
- Pepper to taste
- Scallion Oil (*Mỡ Hành Lá*)*

Serve with:

- Mung bean sprouts (*giá*)
- Aromatic Herb Platter (*Diã Rau Sống*)*
- Cucumber
- Crushed toasted peanuts
- *Nước Mắm* Dip (*Nước Mắm Pha*)*
- Scallion Oil (*Mỡ Hành Lá*)*
- Rice Noodles (*Bún*)*
- Chili purée

This is a variant of the classic Sautéed Beef with Lemongrass (*Bò Xào Sả*)*, but this time the meat is grilled. In Vietnam, since beef is expensive, it is cut into very small pieces, which are then tightly threaded onto skewers.

As in the past, street vendors carry little coal stoves and cook the skewers on demand, spreading an irresistible aroma of grilled meat and scallions all around.

1. Cut the meat into thin strips (2 in x 1 in x 1/16 in).

2. Chop the lemongrass: First discard the hard ends and, if necessary, the dry outer leaves, and then slice thinly. Chop again as finely as possible with a little food processor.

3. Sprinkle salt on the meat, spreading it well, pepper it, and add the lemongrass. Mix, and then thread fairly tightly on skewers. Daub with Scallion Oil*.

4. Grill the skewers over high heat.

In individual bowls, place in this order:
  - A dozen mung bean sprouts
  - One lettuce leaf, filled with herbs, rolled up and cut into 1/8-inch-thick slices
  - A handful of cooked rice noodles

On the top, put side by side:
  - Some cooked beef
  - A few cucumber slices
  - One tablespoon of Scallion Oil*

Sprinkle with a teaspoon of crushed peanuts and 1 or 2 tablespoons of *Nước Mắm* Dip*. You can add a bit of chili purée for taste and color.

REMARKS

In some Vietnamese restaurants, you'll find pieces of meat that are as big as your hand. This is not right: the pieces should be around 2 inches x 1 inch at the most.

The street vendors cut the cucumber by making parallel cuts lengthwise, and then slicing crosswise to produce little matchsticks.

You can serve pork skewers (*Bún Chả*)* in the same manner.

Grilled Beef Rolls in Lót Leaves
Bò Lá Lốt

This dish is one component of the famous *bò bảy món* (seven-course beef) of South Vietnam. *Lá lốt* lends the meat a sweet aroma and prevents it from drying out. If unavailable, grape leaves can be substituted, but they are tougher and definitely don't offer the same flavor.

Serves 6 ~ ⧗ ⧗ ⧗

- 2 lb tender beef
  (figure 5 to 7 oz per serving)
- 2 bunches wild betel leaves (*lá lốt*)
- 1 shallot
- 5 tablespoons pure fish sauce (*nước mắm*)
  or soy sauce (*xì dầu*)
- ½ teaspoon pepper
- 1 heaping teaspoon sugar
- 1 tablespoon peanut oil
- 1 heaping tablespoon wheat flour

1. Cut the beef into the thinnest possible slices (less than 1/16 inch thick), across the grain of the meat.

2. Chop the shallot into very small bits. Wash the *lót* leaves, and then dry carefully. Separate the leaves from the stems and, if possible, let them air-dry some more.

3. Combine the beef, shallot, fish sauce (or soy sauce), pepper, sugar, and oil. Then, finally, sprinkle flour all over and mix well. It is not necessary to let it sit (they even say that seasoned beef hardens and therefore must be used quickly).

4. Start with a leaf, shiny side down. On top, put 2 or 3 pieces of beef. Roll, not too tightly, and place on a tray with the opening facing down so it won't unroll.

5. Grill over high heat, again with the open side on the grill. Both leaf and beef cook rapidly: as soon as the leaf softens and browns, turn it over delicately, grill the other side, and take it off.

Serve with steamed rice vermicelli, Rice Noodles*, or Steamed Rice*. Since the meat is already seasoned, no additional dipping sauce is required. However, if served with rice noodles, the custom dictates that the noodles be presented with *Nước Mắm* Dip*.

REMARKS

If you fear that the meat may be dry, mix a tablespoon of Scallion Oil* with the meat before rolling it in the leaves.

An alternative is to use ground beef (it is also easier to roll). It is also good with duck breast.

You don't have to worry that the roll is tight enough, since, when cooking, the leaf has a tendency to shrink and stick to the meat.

You can use fish sauce as well as soy sauce for seasoning.

Beef Fondue

Bò Nhúng Dấm

This is the simplest Vietnamese "fondue," and the easiest to prepare. Traditionally, it is not served with *nước mắm*, but with *mắm nêm* instead, a sauce made with preserved fish the size of a little finger, strong, yet succulent.

In the South, a bit of coconut milk is added to the broth, but not in the North. Avoid making the broth too acidic: the vinegar is there just for seasoning, not for providing the liquid.

- Beef: tender, lean cut (7 oz per person)

For the broth:
- Chicken or Pork Stock (*Nước Lèo*)*
- 2 teaspoons pitted tamarind (*me*)
- 1 onion cut into thick slices
- 1 or 2 tablespoons white vinegar
- 1 scant teaspoon sugar
- 1 scant teaspoon good curry powder or paste
- 2 tablespoons coconut milk (*nước cốt dừa*), optional
- Salt, pepper

Serve with:
- Aromatic Herb Platter (*Diã Rau Sống*)*
- Rice paper sheets (*bánh tráng*)
- *Mắm Nêm* Dip (*Mắm Nêm Pha*)*
  or else *Mắm Tôm* Dip (*Mắm Tôm Pha*)*
  or possibly *Nước Mắm* Dip (*Nước Mắm Pha*)*

1. Cut the beef into wide and very thin slices, slicing across the grain. In order to get the thinnest slices possible, leave the meat in the freezer for a few hours to harden it (without completely freezing it, though).

2. Boil the tamarind in a half glass of water over very low heat for about 10 minutes. Filter. (Discard the pulp, keep the water!)

3. Add all the ingredients, including the tamarind water but excluding the meat, into the broth. As for the vinegar, add it a little bit at a time, tasting as you go. Season with salt and pepper. The broth should be light and feature a bit of each aroma: go easy on the coconut and the curry powder.

In the middle of the table, place the meat, the rice paper sheets, a bowl of water for dipping them, the herbs, and the broth on its tabletop heater. Serve the *Mắm Nêm* Dip* in small individual bowls.

Soak the rice paper and put lettuce and herbs on it. Cook the meat by plunging it briefly in the broth. Then roll it in the rice paper, dip it in the sauce, and enjoy!

You can also use shrimp, chicken breast, cuttlefish, scallops...

REMARKS

You can, of course, prepare the broth ahead of time. The tamarind is not a traditional ingredient, but it contributes a pleasant taste to the broth.

You can add a bit of liquid to the fondue pot as the broth evaporates. Afterwards, the broth is generally not consumed, unlike that of *Cù Lao*, as it is too strong.

Sautéed Beef with Onions
Bò Xào Củ Hành

This is an everyday dish, in the same league as the ubiquitous pork in caramel sauce *(thịt kho)*. However, as beef is expensive in Vietnam, it is less present than other meats.

A variant *(Bò Xào Sả *)* used in rolls *(Bò Cuốn *)* is seasoned with fish sauce and finely minced lemongrass.

Serves 6 ~ ⧗

- 2 lb tender beef
- 4 tablespoons soy sauce (*xì dầu*)
- 2 level teaspoons sugar
- 2 heaping tablespoons wheat flour
- Pepper

For sautéing:

- ½ onion
- 4 tablespoons peanut oil

1. Slice the meat thinly (¹⁄₁₆ inch or less), cutting across the grain.

2. Combine all the ingredients and knead a little so the meat can soak the flavors.

3. Mince the onion (slicing rather than dicing) and sauté in the oil.

4. Turn the heat to maximum, add in the meat, and stir rapidly. Turn off the heat when cooked to taste.

5. Serve garnished with cilantro leaves or sliced scallions.

REMARK

The flour helps tenderize the meat. However, it is best not to add it too early, as the juice from the meat will create lumps. In general, we mix the flour in just before cooking.

Sautéed Beef with Lemongrass
Bò Xào Sả

Here is a variant of the "everyday" sautéed beef. It is seasoned with finely chopped lemongrass and fish sauce instead of soy sauce. If you want to use it to make rolls, replace the fish sauce with salt, since the roll will be dipped in *nước mắm* at the table.

With the same seasoning, you can make skewers to be served with rice noodles and an aromatic herb platter. Although they are becoming rarer, in Vietnam, you can still see vendors roaming the streets, carrying, on opposite ends of a balanced shoulder rod, a charcoal grill and raw skewers ready to be cooked on demand.

Serves 6 ~ ⧗ ⧗

For preparing the meat:

- 2 lb tender beef
- 2 stalks fresh lemongrass (*sả*, to yield 5 tablespoons of minced lemongrass)
- 4 tablespoons pure fish sauce (*nước mắm*) or 1 teaspoon salt
- 2 level teaspoons sugar
- 2 heaping tablespoons wheat flour
- Pepper

For sautéing:

- 4 tablespoons peanut oil
- 2 shallots (or ½ onion)

1. Chop the lemongrass very finely: first discard the hard ends and also the outside leaves if they are dry, and then cut the stalk into very thin slices. Chop these up finer still, using a food processor if available.

2. Slice the meat thinly (¹⁄₁₆ inch or less), cutting across the grain.

3. Combine all the ingredients with the meat and knead well. If you are planning to make rolls, use salt (but very little, about 1 teaspoon) instead of fish sauce. Let the meat absorb the flavors.

4. Mince the shallots (or onion) and sauté them in the oil.

5. Turn the heat up to maximum and add the meat. Stir it quickly and remove from heat when the meat is barely cooked.

Serve sprinkled with chopped cilantro or scallions.

REMARKS

For the rolls, seasoning isn't that important, since they will be eaten with *Nước Mắm* Dip*, so don't overdo it. Better less than too much!

Turn off the heat when the meat is still pink, as it will continue to cook for a bit.

Pork Skewers and Rice Noodles
Bún Chả

In Vietnam, this dish is sold by street peddlers who carry a shoulder rod with food on one end and a charcoal grill on the other. In the market, shoppers surround them to eat a bite before going on with their business. There are also vendors wandering the streets shouting, "Who wants some *bún chả?*" They set shop in front of people's homes, heat up their grills, and while the skewers are cooking, put out a large woven tray with rice noodles, salad leaves, herbs, and a bowl of *nước mắm* dip in the center. As soon as the skewers are ready, they are placed on the noodles and the tray is presented to the customer.

The ingredients used here are suitable to marinate any cut of pork meat, in particular spareribs.

Serves 5 ~ ⏳ ⏳

- 2 large shallots
- 1 tablespoon sugar
- 5 tablespoons pure fish sauce (*nước mắm*)
- 1 teaspoon fine ground pepper
- 2 lb pork (lean loin or shoulder)

Serve with:

- Rice Noodles (*Bún*)*
  and Scallion Oil (*Mỡ Hành Lá*)*
- Aromatic Herb Platter (*Diã Rau Sống*)*
- *Nước Mắm* Dip (*Nước Mắm Pha*)*

1. Dice the shallots very finely.

2. Cut the meat into bite-sized pieces: make slices ¹⁄₁₆-inch thick across the grain. (Never cut pork into cubes.)

3. Mix all the ingredients thoroughly so the meat is completely coated with the spices. Let marinate for half a day or more.

4. Thread the meat loosely onto the skewers.

5. Grill on a barbecue or electric grill, but definitely not in the oven!

Serve with rice noodles, a platter of fresh herbs, and *Nước Mắm* Dip*.

In North Vietnam, *bún cha* is served together with meatballs seasoned in the same way. Each guest has a large bowl of (not too salty) fish sauce dip in which they plunge the burning-hot meat as soon as it's taken off the grill.

REMARKS

Buy the AUTHENTIC fish sauce *"Nước Mắm Phú Quốc 35°,"* and check that the bottle really says "Product of Vietnam." Beware of imitations!

Marinated meat is best, but if you are in a hurry, you can also cook it immediately.

This dish works well for a barbecue with friends. Though it has a long preparation time, it is not difficult and the work will be finished by the time the guests arrive.

Fried Fish

Cá Chiên

Serves 2 ~ ⧖

- 1 sea bream
- 2 red chili peppers
- 1 stalk fresh lemongrass (*sả*)
- ½ tablespoon salt
- Oil for frying
- 1 small piece of ginger (*gừng*), optional
- *Nước Mắm* Dip (*Nước Mắm Pha*)*, optional

For this popular everyday dish, you can use all sorts of fish, as long as they are fairly wide and not too flat or too thick. In Vietnam, we love little catfish (like *cá trê,* which is always cooked with ginger), or snakehead fish fillets *(cá lóc),* or the recently introduced tilapia *(cá rô phi).* Sea bream also works very well for this type of cooking.

1. Wash and finely chop the chili peppers.

2. Remove the hard ends of the lemongrass stalks. Discard any dry outer leaves. Cut the stalk into thin slices, then chop as finely as possible with a knife or better, a food processor.

3. Wash the fish. Cut off the fins, but leave the head. Gut the fish without opening the belly too much. Scrape the interior clean with a sharp knife. Dry well and make fairly deep diagonal cuts on the side (about ⅛ inch).

4. Combine ½ tablespoon salt, 1 tablespoon chopped lemongrass, and ½ tablespoon chopped chili. Put some of this in each of the incisions and then baste the entire fish.

5. Heat oil in a frying pan, ½-inch deep. Fry the fish over medium heat until the skin is golden brown and crispy (5 to 10 minutes on each side, depending on the thickness of the fish).

Serve immediately with Steamed Rice*. Traditionally (or perhaps by taste), this dish is never served with rice noodles.

REMARK

You can also fry the fish as is, without coating it with the spices. In this case, crush some finely chopped ginger in a garlic press and mix it with some *Nước Mắm* Dip* (some use pure fish sauce). Pour this all over the fish as soon as it comes out of the skillet.

Steamed Fish

Cá Hấp

Serves 2 ~ ⏳⏳

- 1 sea bream, sea bass or red snapper
- 2 oz mung bean thread (*miến*)
- 6 shiitake mushrooms (*nấm hương*)
- 2-inch piece of ginger (*gừng*)
- 3 scallions (*hành lá*)
- 1 shallot
- 2 tablespoons fermented black beans (*tương hột đen*)
- 1 tablespoon peanut oil
- ½ teaspoon sesame oil

Turbot would be the best choice here, but because this large fish is rare and expensive, sea bream is often substituted. Sea bass also works well. This recipe, which showcases the quality and freshness of the ingredients, is probably of Chinese origin.

1. Soak the mung bean thread several hours in advance, together with the shiitake mushrooms, if they are dried.

2. Prepare the garnish:
   - Cut the ginger into thin strands
   - Cut the scallions into 2-inch segments
   - Mince the shallot not too finely
   - Drain the mushrooms by pressing them, and then cut into little slices about 1/16-inch thick

3. Wash and dry the fish. For turbot, make an incision along its dorsal fin and lift the flesh on each side without separating it entirely. Slide some shallot and ginger into the two pockets (or into the belly for the sea bream and sea bass).

4. Put the bean thread at the bottom of a baking dish so it can soak up the sauce. Place the fish on top and then cover with the other ingredients in this order: shallots, ginger, scallion, and black beans. Arrange the mushrooms on the side. Sprinkle with peanut oil or the oil from the black beans.

5. Steam for about ½ hour depending on the size of the fish. (If the fish is too big, cover and seal it with parchment paper and cook in the oven at 425 °F). Sprinkle with sesame oil. Serve with Steamed Rice*.

Fish in Caramel Sauce
Cá Kho

This dish and its many
variants are eaten routinely
in all the Vietnamese homes.

The fine and succulent *cá loc* is often
used, its head and tail carefully reserved
for making Sour Soup with Fish *(Canh Chua)**.
By combining *cá kho* and *canh chua,* a full meal can be
obtained out of a single fish. This was frequently the
case in the old days in the countryside. Small thumb-
sized fish that cook rapidly are also used with the same
type of preparation *(cá rô, cá bong).*

Serves 4 ~ ⏳⏳

- 2 lb oily fish with a round or oval cross
  section (big mackerel, *cá lóc, cá bông lau*)
- 3 scallions *(hành lá)*
- ½ teaspoon pepper
- 1 teaspoon sugar
- 4 tablespoons pure fish sauce *(nước mắm)*
- 1 heaping tablespoon sugar
  (for the caramel)

Outside Vietnam—all the Vietnamese cooks know
it—the lowly mackerel gives you the best results for this
dish. Paradoxically, mackerel is unknown in Vietnam.
On the other hand, salmon doesn't work (too smelly),
nor does hake (too soft), or tuna (too dry).

Classic Method

1. Wash, scale, and gut the fish. Remove the head. Cut the body into 1-inch sections.

   Preparing mackerel requires a little care: after cutting off the head, gut the fish through the top, without opening the belly, otherwise the flesh may come apart when cooking. Using a small knife, scrape the cavity to remove the blood that sticks to the sides, and then rinse under a jet of water. The inside must be white.

3. Pour onto the fish and allow it to marinate for at least 1 hour.

5. Place the fish pieces in a single layer in the saucepan containing the caramel. It's best if they are pressed one against the other, especially if the bellies are sliced open, to prevent them from crumbling. Pour the marinade on top, up to the level of the fish.

7. Toward the end, you can turn up the heat for 10 minutes to reduce the volume of liquid, until you get a thick and somewhat viscous sauce. Taste and adjust the seasoning with pure fish sauce and a bit of sugar and pepper.

2. Chop and crush 2 or 3 scallions. Mix with the pepper, the sugar (one teaspoon only), and the pure fish sauce.

4. In a large saucepan, prepare a clear caramel with 1 heaping tablespoon of sugar and ½ tablespoon of water. When the caramel is ready, pour in ½ cup of water and turn off the heat.

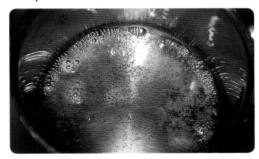

6. Bring to a boil, then set the heat on low and cover. After 10 minutes, lower the heat so that it's barely boiling. Simmer for 3 hours. The level of the liquid shouldn't drop too much.

Serve with rice and possibly a soup (*Canh Chua**) made with the head and tail of the *cá lóc* (but not the head and tail of a mackerel)!

REMARKS

This dish shouldn't be all that salty. Don't use too much sugar either, sweet fish tastes terrible!

A cast iron casserole works perfectly for this type of slow, gentle cooking.

Simplified Cá Kho

Prepare the caramel as in the Classic Method*. Clean and cut the fish, skipping the marinade part. Pack the fish into the saucepan, add salt and sugar, and then the caramel. Simmer 2 to 3 hours as in the Classic Method.

Add pure fish sauce only at the end, and adjust the seasoning with a little sugar and pepper. This technique has the considerable advantage of limiting the odors of fish sauce during the cooking.

Cá Kho Tộ

A *tộ* is a large terracotta bowl, larger and more rustic than a soup bowl (*tô*). *Cá Kho Tộ* is generally prepared with a very fatty fish, the result being a bit caramelized. The sauce, as rich as you could desire, is delectable when poured atop steamed rice.

Select, therefore, a fatty fish, such as catfish or mackerel. Cut it in slices ½-inch thick. Use it to prepare *cá kho* as in the Classic Method*, but cook it on higher heat: the fish will caramelize quite fast. Continue cooking until there is practically no liquid left, just a thick reddish sauce. It is the custom to use a little more sugar and pepper than for regular *cá kho*.

You can, at the same time, put a ½-inch-thick slice of pork belly in the pot. The fat from the meat adds to that of the fish, which might otherwise be insufficient.

This dish has a stronger taste than regular *cá kho*. It is very popular and gets even better if refrigerated and then reheated: the fish will only become firmer.

Cá Kho Xổi

This is a sort of instant *cá kho* made with softer fish (hake, halibut, or flounder) than those normally used for *cá kho*. Unlike the preceding method, there is no need to simmer for hours. The result is good, though the fish does not soak up the sauce as much as in the other methods.

Marinate as in the Classic Method* using a mix of fish sauce, scallions, pepper, and sugar. Prepare a clear caramel and add 1 cup of water. When the caramel boils again, put in the fish, whole or in fillets. Let it boil long enough to

cook the fish, then adjust the seasoning to taste. If needed, add 1 or 2 chili peppers when you turn off the heat.

The dish will be a bit more liquid than regular *cá kho*. It should be in between *canh* and *cá kho*, more salty and dense than *canh*, but less than *cá kho*.

Serve with Rice Noodles (*Bún*)*: place the noodles in individual bowls, pour some sauce over, and eat with the fish.

Pan Dried Fish

Cá Xấy

We don't know for sure where this dish came from, but it's a very convenient and tasty way to recycle leftover *Cá Kho**. Oddly and luckily enough, the fish loses its strong smell in the process.

1. Remove the bones if necessary. For mackerel, you can leave them: after cooking, they will become brittle and can be eaten like those of sardines.

3. Add the fish sauce and sugar. Keep crushing and stirring until the fish becomes dry and no more steam comes out. Cook it a few minutes beyond that, then turn off the heat. You get a kind of coarse *thịt chà bong*.

Serves 2 ~ ⧖

- 1 cup leftover cooked fish (*Cá Kho** or other)
- 2 cloves garlic
- 2 or 3 tablespoons peanut oil
- 1 scant tablespoon pure fish sauce (*nước mắm*)
- ½ teaspoon sugar

2. Sauté the crushed garlic in hot oil. When it is barely turning golden, add the fish. Using a spatula or fork, crush the fish, stirring constantly over high (but not too high) heat for 10 minutes.

Serve with rice. The dish should be only slightly salty, but not bland.

Baked Whole Fish
Cá Nướng Trui

This dish was born in South Vietnam under specific circumstances: in the harvest season, thieves would often come to cut and steal the ripe rice. Thus, two or three men would stay out all night in the fields to keep watch. To pass the time, they fished and then cooked and ate the fish on the spot, sitting on one of the little dams that separate the submerged rice paddies.

One method was to wrap the fish in clay, scales, innards, and all, and put the whole package on the fire. When they broke the clay crust, it would take the scales and skin with it. Rice paper sheets and *mắm* were brought along to accompany this fish, which could not be fresher. The feast would sometimes be helped along with a few sips of rice wine.

Owing to its traditional origin, this dish is still very popular today. In spite of its elaborate looks, it is fairly easy to prepare.

Serves 4 ~ ⏳

- 1 large whole fish (3 lb), for example sea bass, sea bream, or red snapper
- ⅓ cup Scallion Oil (*Mỡ Hành Lá*)*

Serve with:

- Aromatic Herb Platter (*Dĩa Rau Sống*)*
- *Mắm Nêm* Dip (*Mắm Nêm Pha*)*
- Rice paper sheets (*bánh tráng*)
- Fresh cucumber
- Pickled Vegetables (*Đồ Chua*)*, optional

1. Pick a very fresh whole fish. There is no need to empty and clean its cavity. Wrap it in parchment paper and put it on a baking sheet.

2. Place in an oven preheated to 400 °F. The cooking time depends on the size of the fish: as an indication, figure about 30 minutes for 3 lb.

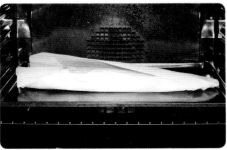

3. Remove the paper (with a bit of luck, the skin will peel off with it), place the fish on a serving plate, and baste it with Scallion Oil*.

4. Serve accompanied with the traditional salad and herb platter, rice paper sheets, sliced cucumbers, and pickles. Serve the *Mắm Nêm* Dip* in little individual bowls.

Each guest takes a rice paper sheet, dips it quickly in water, and makes it into a small roll filled with some salad leaves, herbs, and fish. Then they dip the roll in the *Mắm Nêm* Dip* before enjoying it.

REMARKS

Nowadays, even in Vietnam, people no longer catch *cá lóc* in the rice paddies, but they buy it instead. Abroad, you can choose from many different types of fish like sea bass or sea bream. You can also find frozen *cá lóc*. You will need to choose a large enough fish, because the head and the backbone are big.

You can leave the skin on the fish. Some people like to eat it.

Traditionally, *bún* is not served with this dish, but you can bet your guests will request some!

Meat Curry

Cà-Ri

Indian immigrants to Vietnam used to cook *cà-ri* with goat meat. Vietnamese people prefer chicken or beef, sometimes adding bits of carrot (although it used to be an expensive vegetable, as it wouldn't grow anywhere except in Dalat) or potatoes. You can also use eggplants: they make the sauce thicker and richer.

Serves 6 ~ ⧖ ⧖

- 1 chicken, cut into pieces (or 3 lb beef stew meat)
- 6 cloves garlic, crushed
- 1 large onion, finely chopped
- 3 tablespoons curry powder or paste
- 1 eggplant, 4 potatoes, 2 carrots (optional)
- 1 cup coconut milk (*nước cốt dừa*), optional
- 2 tablespoons oil
- 4 bay leaves (laurel)
- Salt

1. In a large bowl, place the chicken, crushed garlic, onion and curry. Sprinkle with a bit of salt. Mix well, cover, and let sit half a day or overnight (you can also cook it immediately; however, the dish is best when the meat has time to soak up the spices).

2. Heat 2 tablespoons of oil in a heavy cooking pot. Brown the meat a bit. Add the crumpled bay leaves, cubed eggplant, and a little water without drowning the meat: the water should come up to about half the height of the meat pieces.

3. Lower the heat, cover, and let simmer: 1 or 2 hours for beef, less (30 minutes) for chicken, as it cooks faster. Add the carrots and large potato cubes in the middle of the cooking time for beef, or right at the beginning for chicken. When finished, you will get a rather thick sauce; if not, reduce it by turning up the heat.

4. Optional: at the end of the cooking, add the coconut milk: 1 cup to obtain a sauce that is light enough to eat with rice noodles. For a thicker sauce, use only the top fatty part of the coconut can.

The creamy top of the coconut can

5. Season to taste with salt and optionally additional curry mix. *Cà-ri* being always a spicy dish, feel free to add chili peppers to taste.

Serve with rice or Rice Noodles (*Bún*)*. Many Vietnamese are in the habit of eating this with bread, soaking up the sauce with enthusiasm.

REMARKS

Like in most Vietnamese dishes, the meat should be cut into pieces small enough to be seized with chopsticks and eaten without requiring a knife.

We prefer Indian curry. It is more sophisticated than occidental curry or the Southeast Asian type.

Fish Skewers with Turmeric
Chả Cá

These skewers, originating from North Vietnam, are traditionally grilled over a wood fire, but it is easier to cook them on a barbecue or, if unavailable, an electric grill. This is a dish everyone likes, but it is costly, as you need a lot of the best cuts of very fresh fish. Monkfish is the top choice, but less expensive fish will work as well. If you can find it, catfish (*cá bông lau*) produces an equally excellent result.

The North Vietnamese people always add one or two drops of essence of mangdana (*cà cuống*) in their *mắm tôm*. Those in the South, on the other hand, are much less fond of it!

Galanga is a rhizome similar to ginger. Vietnamese dill has a shorter stalk and a more sustained flavor than its occidental cousin. Fried dried shallots can be found in all Asian supermarkets.

Serves 5 ~ ⏳⏳⏳

- 2 lb fish fillet with firm flesh (monkfish or catfish for example)
- 2-inch piece of galanga (*riềng*)
- 1 bunch Vietnamese dill (*thìa là*)
- 1 shallot (optional)
- 1 heaping tablespoon shrimp paste (*mắm tôm*)
- 1 heaping tablespoon turmeric powder (*nghệ*)
- 1 + 5 tablespoons oil
- 3 tablespoons fried shallots (*hành phi*)

Serve with:

- Aromatic Herb Platter (*Dĩa Rau Sống*)*
- Rice Noodles (*Bún*)*
- 5 scallions (*hành lá*)
- 1 cup whole toasted peanuts
- 1 cup *Mắm Tôm* Dip (*Mắm Tôm Pha*)*
- Chilli pepper

1. Cut the galanga into strands with a knife, or chop it with a machine. Finely chop the shallots and half of the dill in a food processor.

2. Cut the fish into pieces roughly 1½ x 1 x ½ inch. Season with the chopped dill, galanga, shallots, shrimp paste, turmeric, and 1 tablespoon of oil. Mix well.

3. Allow to marinate several hours, then either thread the pieces onto skewers or leave separate, depending on how you will cook them.

4. Grill the fish over high heat: it cooks rapidly. Turn over when halfway done. Watch that the pieces don't fall apart. Best to use a nonstick grill.

5. In a small saucepan, heat 5 tablespoons of oil. Toss in the fried shallots and turn off the heat immediately.

6. Wash the rest of the dill and cut into ½-inch pieces, tossing out the hard base of the stalks.

7. Remove the fish from the skewers and place on a serving platter. Cover with the rest of the dill. Pour the fried shallots with their hot oil on top.

Serve immediately, while the fish is still very hot. The table should have already been set with the platter of aromatic herbs, the rice noodles, a small bowl with the white parts of the scallions split lengthwise in four, another bowl of whole toasted peanuts, a bowl of *Mắm Tôm* Dip*, and the chili pepper.

Each guest puts some noodles in a bowl, then some herbs, peanuts, scallions, and a piece of fish, and then pours a spoonful of *mắm tôm* sauce on top.

REMARK

Use raw peanuts and toast them yourself rather than buying the roasted and salted ones. You can also fry the shallots yourself.

Pork Patties with Green Rice
Chả Cốm

Gạo nếp is a special type of rice, commonly known as "sticky rice." A more exact designation would be "glutinous rice." Green rice *(cốm dẹp)* is made from glutinous rice harvested before maturity, when the grains are still green, and then toasted rapidly and flattened. It has a particular scent which, unfortunately, disappears with time.

The dish presented here is typical in the North. Nowadays, since you can find dried green rice in Asian markets, you can prepare this dish at any time of the year. Previously, you had to wait until the harvest season to find the tender rice.

Serves 4 ~ ⧖ ⧖

- 1 lb ground pork shoulder
- 5 oz + 2 oz green rice *(cốm dẹp)*
- 3 teaspoons pure fish sauce *(nước mắm)*
- 3 teaspoons pepper

1. Mix all the ingredients well (don't forget to reserve 2 oz of glutinous rice for a later step). Press the mixture with a spoon to make it compact, and leave it in the refrigerator for several hours or even half a day, so that the rice has time to soften.

2. Divide into 8 balls and flatten by pressing them between two boards. Press and smooth to fix up the edges.

3. Steam the patties for 10 minutes.

4. Cover each patty with a layer of the reserved dry green rice. Press well so that the rice grains don't fall off.

5. Fry for 1 minute on each side so that you get a crispy outside and a moist interior.

Serve the patties with rice. You can also cut them into smaller slices and serve them as an appetizer.

REMARKS

The patties should be the size of a small hamburger: if bigger, they are difficult to cook, if smaller, the meat might be too dry.

After steaming, the patties can be frozen and kept for a long time. Thus you only need fry them before serving.

Stuffed Crab
Chả Cua Nhồi

Serves 12 ~ ⏳⏳⏳⏳

- 3 large crabs
  (or 1½ lb crab meat)

- 3 large slices of sweet
  white bread (brioche or
  hotdog bun)

- 3 shallots (preferably)
  or 1 onion

- 1 lb ground pork shoulder

- 2 eggs

- 2 tablespoons pure
  fish sauce (*nước mắm*)

- 1 generous teaspoon
  pepper

This dish, which has roots in both French and Vietnamese cuisine, is expensive and labor intensive, so it is reserved for special occasions. It is quite similar to the traditional *Chả Cua**, but with a different aroma, since it is baked whereas *Chả Cua* is steamed.

One crab is enough for four people, as the dish is, after all, fairly heavy.

1. Cook the crabs in boiling water for 20 minutes, then shell them completely, legs included, and pick all the meat. Above all, don't throw away the shells!

2. Clean the shells well, brushing them inside and out. Let dry. You can reuse the shells after washing them in the dishwasher.

3. Toast the bread, then make breadcrumbs using a food processor. You can also buy packaged breadcrumbs, but homemade toasted buttery breadcrumbs taste much better!

4. Chop the shallots very finely with a knife (not with a food processor: this would crush them and produce shallot juice). Shallots are preferred over onions for their aroma.

5. Grind the meat if necessary. If it's too lean, you can add 1 or 2 tablespoons of peanut oil.

6. Mix all the ingredients well. Season with the fish sauce and pepper. The stuffing should be fairly sticky and compact; if not, add a bit of egg, some meat, or a little oil. You will have enough to stuff 4 crab shells.

7. Oil the insides of the shells. Pack the stuffing firmly into the shells using a spoon. Alternatively, you can use a ceramic pâté mold (terrine).

Cook in the oven (375 °F) for 35 minutes. Let it cool slightly. Serve by itself, or with steamed rice, or possibly some bread.

REMARKS

You need a good half-hour to pick the meat from one crab. If fresh crab is unavailable, use frozen Canadian crab, sold in 1 lb blocks.

This dish freezes readily. Before serving, reheat it in a medium oven for 15 minutes without thawing first. Keep an eye on it so it doesn't dry out.

In certain months—October for example—crabs carry eggs. If this is the case, crumble the eggs and disperse them in the stuffing. You'll get a very pleasant result: the pâté will be dotted with pretty orange bits.

Shrimp Cake

Chả Tôm

Even though shrimp was not really that expensive in the past, *chả tôm* remained a special dish that one would prepare for the Lunar New Year or an ancestor's anniversary. It is served as an appetizer or, in Central Vietnam, accompanied by *banh lá*.

It can also be eaten as a main course with rice, but then be sure to surround it with other delicacies, not a common *thịt kho* or *canh chua!* Its preparation is delicate: the heat must not be too high, nor must it cook for too long.

For 4 cakes ~ ⏳⏳

- 1 lb medium-sized shelled shrimp
- 1 scant teaspoon sugar
- 1 tablespoon potato starch
- 1 tablespoon pure fish sauce (*nước mắm*)
- ½ clove garlic (optional)
- 1 egg
- 1 scant teaspoon baking powder
- A few cilantro leaves (*ngò*)

1. Wash, devein, and dry the shrimp. Add the sugar, starch, pure fish sauce, and optionally the garlic. Mix well in a food processor until the paste becomes almost white. Place in the freezer for half an hour.

4. Steam 20 minutes over low heat (if too hot, the paste will puff up, and the cake will be ruined). Check the cooking progress by poking it with a knife. Make sure condensation doesn't drip onto the top surface of the cake; if it does, the cake won't look nice. You can stretch a porous fabric such as cheesecloth over the mold to catch water dripping from the lid. You can also use a mold that does not let water through (as in the photo below).

Let it cool before unmolding, and then decorate with cilantro leaves. Slice into bite-sized diamonds or squares.

Serve cold or slightly warm, as an appetizer or as a main course with rice or soup (*canh*).

2. Get the mix out of the freezer; add ½ egg white (reserve the yolk) and the baking powder. Again, mix well using the food processor.

3. Pour into a cake mold (about 8 inches in diameter, oiled unless it is nonstick) to a thickness of about ⅔ inch. Smooth the whole surface carefully, pressing with the back of a spoon, paying particular attention to the edges.

5. Beat the egg yolk with two drops of pure fish sauce, and use to baste the top of the cake. Let the cake brown a tiny bit in the oven, making sure that it doesn't dry out: it will take on an appetizing reddish-orange color.

REMARKS

For a nice-looking cake, take care to pack the mix well, especially around the edges, then smooth the surface by passing the back of a spoon to and fro.

Although they are ground to a paste, you still need fairly large shrimp for the cake to have a good consistency: if the shrimp are too small, the cake will be less crunchy. Don't add too much baking powder: one teaspoon is enough.

Shrimp Balls
Chạo Tôm

This dish from the South is a kind of deluxe version of *Nem Nướng**, in which shrimp replaces the pork meat. It is tricky to cook: you must first barely steam it, and then fry it exactly so, watching over closely the entire time.

Serves 8 ~ ⌛ ⌛ ⌛

- 2 ¼ lb large shelled shrimp
- 2 teaspoons sugar
- 2 teaspoons potato starch
- 2 teaspoons pure fish sauce (*nước mắm*)
- 4 large cloves garlic, peeled
- 3 oz barding fat
- 1 small egg white
- 2 scant teaspoons baking powder
- Canned sugarcane (*mía*), optional
- Peanut oil

Serve with:

- Rice paper sheets (*bánh tráng*)
- Aromatic Herb Platter (*Diã Rau Sống*)*
- Pickled Vegetables (*Đồ Chua*)*
- *Nước Mắm* Dip (*Nước Mắm Pha*)*
- Rice Noodles (*Bún*)*, optional

Rau giấp cá goes well with shrimp, but beware, not everyone appreciates the unusual fragrance of this very special herb!

1. Wash and devein the shrimp. Dry them well. Add the sugar, potato starch, pure fish sauce, and garlic. Process with an electric mixer until the paste becomes very light in color. Cool in the freezer for a half hour; this will make the balls crunchier.

2. Blanch the barding fat for 1 minute in boiling salted water, drain, and let cool. Dice into tiny cubes (1/10-inch or less).

3. Remove the shrimp mix from the freezer. Add the egg white and the baking powder. Blend well, using an electric mixer. Add the barding fat and mix again, this time by hand.

4. Shape slightly elongated balls the size of a small plum, oiling your hands and pressing well: knead each ball in the palm of your hand for quite a while (to go faster, you can make two at a time, one in each hand).

5. Steam over fairly low heat. If the heat is too high, the balls will puff up, then collapse. When the balls turn pink (it takes between 1 and 2 minutes) remove them immediately.

6. Let the cooked balls cool completely. If necessary, dab them with a paper towel, pressing a bit to sop up any water.

7. Just before serving, fry the balls rapidly in oil that is barely boiling. Take them out before they turn brown, or the outside will be chewy.

Serve with rice paper sheets, a platter of aromatic herbs and pickled vegetables. Although it's not traditional, any time people eat that type of rolls, they request rice noodles. So you might as well have some ready!

Unlike *Nem Nướng**, this is accompanied by *Nước Mắm Dip**, and not peanut sauce.

Resist the temptation to use a large egg white, as it would cause the balls to puff up too much. You should knead each ball by hand at least 50 times so that after cooking its surface will be nice and smooth. With a bit of practice, you can produce 2 lb of balls in 30 minutes.

You can roll the raw shrimp paste around a piece of sugarcane (split lengthwise into sticks the size of a little finger). In this case, after steaming the shrimp balls are not fried, but reheated in the oven before serving.

After steaming, you can freeze the balls. Thaw them slowly, and fry them just before putting them on the table.

A variant: instead of frying the balls, you can dip them in beaten egg holding them with a barbecue skewer, and then steam them or cook them over a flame. Serve as an appetizer.

REMARKS

Strangely enough, even though the shrimp are ground to a paste, size does matter: to get crunchy balls, you need to choose rather large shrimp with grey meat, not white. Watch out: shrimp are not good when cooked for too long!

Stuffed Quail with Green Rice

Chim Cút Nhồi Cốm Dẹp

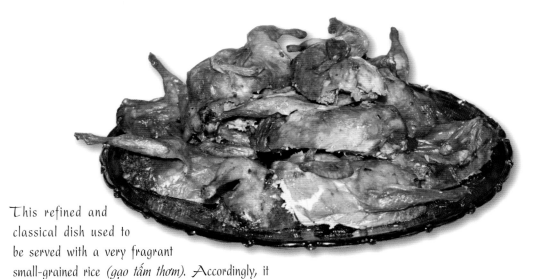

This refined and classical dish used to be served with a very fragrant small-grained rice *(gạo tấm thơm)*. Accordingly, it was expensive fare, reserved for special guests.

Green rice *(cốm dẹp)* is made from glutinous rice *(gạo nếp)* that is harvested before maturity, when the grains are still green. You will find a product sold under the appellation *"cốm dẹp"* everywhere, but unfortunately, most of the time this is just ordinary glutinous rice that has been crushed and colored. It can be used for want of anything better. For now, the real *cốm dẹp* can only be found in Vietnam.

Serves 6 ~ ⧖ ⧖

- 6 quail, gutted and cleaned
- Peanut oil

Stuffing:

- 10 oz ground pork shoulder
- 3 tablespoons green glutinous rice *(cốm dẹp)*
- 1 small shallot, finely chopped
- 2 tablespoons pure fish sauce *(nước mắm)*
- ½ teaspoon pepper

1. Combine all the stuffing ingredients.

2. Thoroughly gut and clean the quail, if they didn't come already cleaned. Dry the skins well to prevent them from boiling when roasting. Fill each bird with stuffing, packing it lightly.

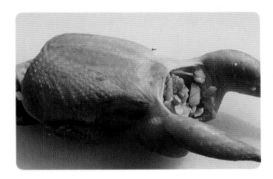

3. Coat the quail lightly with oil and place them belly up on a baking dish.

4. Cook in a preheated oven (425 °F) for about 45 min (for 6 quail).

Enjoy immediately; this dish is significantly less tasty if reheated, or, even worse, if frozen then thawed.

REMARKS

You can season with salt in place of the fish sauce.

If there is leftover stuffing, use it to prepare *Chả Cốm**.

Stir-Fried Chicken with Lemongrass
Gà Xào Sả

In the past, each Vietnamese family raised its own chickens in the backyard, reserving them for special occasions. Chicken meat was expensive and considered a luxury.

Nowadays, commercially produced poultry is common, and this flavorful dish has become as ordinary as steak and fries in a Parisian bistrot.

Serves 4 ~ ⧖ ⧖

- 1 medium chicken
- 1 red chili pepper
- 2 stalks fresh lemongrass (sả)
- ½ teaspoon salt
- 1 heaping tablespoon sugar
- 4 tablespoons oil
- Pepper to taste

1. Discard the hard ends and, if necessary, the dry external leaf of each lemongrass stalk. Cut the stalks into thin slices.

2. Wash the chili pepper and chop it together with the lemongrass as finely as possible, using a food processor, for example.

3. Cut the chicken with the bones into small pieces, at most 2 inches wide. Add the chili pepper and lemongrass mix, the salt, and the sugar. Let marinate a few hours.

Season to taste with salt and pepper. Serve with steamed rice.

4. Heat the oil in a large pan. Cook the chicken pieces over medium heat, uncovered, for around 20 to 25 minutes. Adjust the heat so that the meat does not produce too much juice. At the end of the cooking, turn up the heat. Turn it off as soon as the chicken is browned, so that it doesn't dry out.

REMARKS

Traditionally, lemongrass dishes are seasoned with salt instead of fish sauce.

If chopsticks are used at the table, the chicken must be cut into bite-size pieces. When using Western cutlery, it is best to make bigger pieces to avoid little bones and their dangers.

Vietnamese Fondue
Lẫu Thập Cẩm

This traditional fondue allows you to welcome your guests with a colorful dinner table and treat them to a cheerful, informal meal. This dish is not usually served with rice paper sheets, but with mung bean threads *(miến)* instead. Another indispensable ingredient is *rau tần ô,* also called *cải cúc* in the North.

Serves 12 ~ ⧗ ⧗ ⧗

- 2 qt chicken broth (*Nước Lèo - Nước Dùng*)*

- Seasoning for the broth: tamarind powder (*me*), onion, scallions, cilantro

- 1 lb mung bean threads (*miến*)

- Meats:
  2½ lb tender, lean beef
  1 lb block of tofu
  2½ lb medium-sized shrimp
  1½ lb scallops

- Vegetables:
  rau tần ô: 1 large bunch
  Taro stalk (*bạc hà*, optional): 2 stalks
  Napa cabbage (*cải bắc thảo*): 1
  Chinese broccoli (*cải làn*): 24 stalks
  Enoki mushrooms

- *Nước Mắm* Dip (*Nước Mắm Pha*)*
  Mắm Ruốc Dip (*Mắm Ruốc Pha*)*

1. When the broth is ready, filter it. Season with salt and pepper; add 1 tablespoon tamarind powder, 1 onion cut into 8 pieces, scallions cut into 1-inch-long pieces, and finally the cilantro leaves. Let it boil another 10 minutes.

2. Soak the bean threads in warm water for at least 2 hours. Drain and cut into manageable lengths. Place on a serving platter.

3. Prepare the "protein":
   - Cut the beef into thin slices.
   - Cut the tofu into bite-sized pieces.
   - Peel and clean the shrimp.
   - Prepare the scallops.

The "meat"

4. Wash and present the vegetables on one or several plates:
   - *Rau tần ô* as is.
   - *Bạc hà* cut into diagonal slices ¼-inch thick.
   - *Cải bắc thảo* cut crosswise in 4 (separate the leaves).
   - *Cải làn* cut across in two.

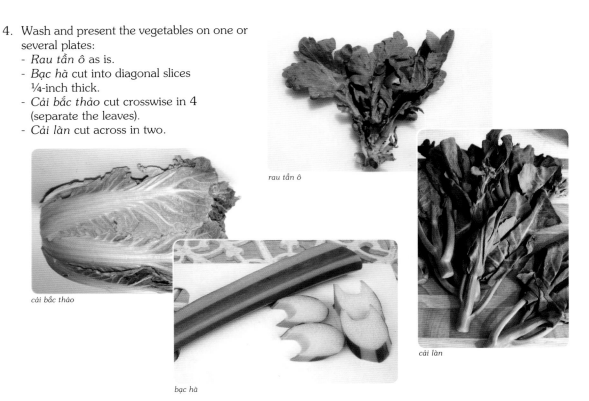

rau tần ô

cải bắc thảo

cải làn

bạc hà

The vegetables

Put all the ingredients on the table and place the broth in the middle on a heater. Guests cook the ingredients of their choice in the broth with the help of a small wire net. You can drink the broth at the end of the dinner.

Serve with *Nước Mắm* Dip* and *Mắm Ruốc* Dip* in small individual bowls.

REMARKS

The tamarind is not traditionally used in this dish, but it pleasantly enhances the taste of the broth. If it is not available, you can substitute vinegar.

You can also serve rice paper sheets (*bánh tráng*) for making rolls, even though it is not traditional either.

It is possible to use frozen raw shrimp. In Vietnam, in place of the scallops, minced chicken breast or squid pieces the size of a finger are used.

You can use other vegetables as long as they don't have too strong a taste. Leeks and cauliflower should be avoided; sugar peas work well.

Don't hesitate to provide a large bunch of *rau tần ô*. It "melts" as soon as it is dipped in the broth, and its presence is crucial.

You can add water little by little as the broth evaporates.

Preserved Fish Pâté
Mắm Chưng

Version 1 ~ ⧗ ⧗ ⧗

- ½ cup ground pork
  (loin or belly without the rind)

- 1 slice preserved snakehead fish (*mắm lóc*),
  with or without the backbone

- ½ teaspoon sugar

- 3 scallions (*hành lá*), cut into 1-inch-long pieces
  or 1 minced shallot

- A few slices ginger (*gừng*, optional)

- A few turns of the pepper grinder

1. Put the meat at the bottom of a bowl, then layer the other ingredients, one on top of the other, in the order of the ingredient list above.

2. Place the bowl in a pot of water so that it is half immersed, bring the water to a gentle boil, and cover. Simmer until the meat is fully cooked (15 to 20 minutes).

Serve with slices of cucumber and cooked pork belly, fresh herbs, and, of course, steamed rice!

Mắm chưng is a kind of meatloaf in which the star ingredient is *mắm lóc,* a preserved fish. It is presented in two forms here. A third way of using *mắm lóc* is *mắm thái thịt luộc.*

This is a dish from the South, in particular from the countryside, where the fish needed to make *mắm* are more than abundant. *Mắm lóc* is prepared with *cá lóc,* a freshwater fish resembling hake. *Mắm lóc* is sold in jars, sometimes thoroughly cleaned, sometimes simply cut into pieces, backbone and all. The best quality has medium-size to large fish, with firm mahogany-colored flesh.

Version 2 ~ ⧖ ⧖ ⧖

- ½ cup carefully cleaned preserved snakehead fish (*mắm lóc*), without any bones or skin
- ½ cup ground pork (loin or belly without the rind)
- 1 egg
- ½ shallot, finely chopped (optional)
- A few turns of the pepper grinder
- 1 egg yolk for basting the top

1. Chop the preserved fish. Mix all the ingredients well (except for the last egg yolk). Pack it all in a small terrine or in a bowl.

2. Cook in a covered double boiler. When the cooking is almost complete, beat the egg yolk and pour it in a layer on top of the pâté. Finish the cooking in the double boiler, still covered, over low heat so the egg does not inflate. All in all, the cooking takes 15 to 30 minutes (stick a knife in to test the consistency of the meat).

Decorate the top of the pâté with flattened cilantro leaves and a few split chili peppers. Serve with slices of cucumber, cooked pork belly, fresh herbs, and rice.

REMARK

Don't season with salt or fish sauce, as the preserved fish is already salty enough.

Preserved Fish Soup
Mắm Kho

Mắm kho is actually a kind of soup prepared with both preserved fish (mắm sặc) and fresh fish.

- Mắm sặc, sold in glass jars, is made with cá sặc, a small flat fish, which is normally eaten fried. The smallest are made into mắm.

- For the fresh fish, cá lóc is used in Vietnam. Catfish, easier to find abroad, also works well.

Serves 8 ~ ⧗ ⧗
- ½ to 1 cup preserved gouramy fish (mắm sặc)
- 2 stalks lemongrass (sả)
- ½ lb pork belly
- 2 small shallots
- 1 lb fresh fish (catfish)
- Sugar (a little bit only)

1. Chop the lemongrass very finely: first by hand, and then with a food processor, reducing it almost to a powder.

2. Cut the pork belly in pieces the size of a little finger or in ½-inch-wide slices. Mince the shallots and sauté them with the meat and a little bit of oil. Add the ground lemongrass, cover, and simmer 15 minutes or so, until the meat is tender.

3. Cut the fresh fish into individual portions. You can also make smaller pieces. When the meat is ready, add the fish to the pan. Wait until it's cooked (around 5 minutes) and turn off the heat.

4. Drain the *mắm sặc*. Simmer it over low heat in 1 quart of water until the meat flakes (around 15 minutes). Filter to get rid of the little bones. Note: it's the cooking broth that we will keep; the rest is thrown out!

5. Pour the cooking broth into a pot and add the fish and pork mix. Ensure that there is about 1 bowl of soup per guest. Adjust the seasoning: add water if too salty and a tiny bit of sugar if necessary.

Serve one of two ways:

- **With rice:** offer a large platter of aromatic herbs, sliced cucumbers, sliced green bananas, sliced star fruit, etc. Pour the *Mắm Kho* into a large common bowl or into little individual bowls. In the latter case, each guest has a bowl of rice and a bowl of *Mắm Kho*.

- **Fondue style:** place a large pot of *Mắm Kho* on a heater in the middle of the table, and on the side, a large pile of greens to be cooked (*rau tần ô, hẹ, rau muống,* and other green vegetables). Each guest dips the greens in the broth and eats them with rice or noodles (*bún*, a recent innovation).

REMARKS

Mắm sặc in jars is very salty. Above all, don't use the liquid from the jar.

Always add a little sugar to sweeten, but very little.

The quantity and quality of garnishes can vary according to what's available in the kitchen.

Grilled Pork Meatballs
Nem Nướng

In Vietnam, although *nem nướng* is served in street eateries, it remains fairly expensive, as it is essentially meat-based. On request, the vendor prepares a platter containing five or six meatballs together with aromatic herbs. It is a treat to be enjoyed as a snack, not as a main meal.

Serves 10 ~ ⧖ ⧖ ⧖

- 3 ½ lb ground pork (not too lean)
- 10 cloves garlic
- 5 oz barding fat (optional)
- 4 tablespoons cold water
- 2 tablespoons roasted rice flour (*thính*)
- 3 tablespoons sugar
- 2 teaspoons salt
- 1 teaspoon baking powder
- 2 tablespoons potato starch or tapioca starch

Serve with:

- Raw garlic cloves
- Chinese chives (*hẹ*)
- Rice paper (*bánh tráng*)
- Aromatic Herb Platter (*Diã Rau Sống*)*
- Peanut Sauce (*Tương Pha*)*

1. Peel the garlic cloves and grind them in a food processor, as finely as possible. You can also crush them using a mortar and pestle or a garlic press.

3. Combine all the ingredients with the ground pork. Mix well.

5. Grill the meatballs over medium heat (not too hot so the inside has time to cook), turning over halfway through cooking. This will take about 15 minutes.

2. Place the barding fat in boiling water for 30 to 60 seconds until it becomes translucent, then dice it finely (1/16-inch-wide cubes).

4. Form oblong balls about the size of a large olive, oiling your hands and pressing firmly. It's said that you must knead each ball 50 times so it doesn't fall apart (to go faster, use both hands and make 2 balls at once).

Serve with: rice paper sheets, herbs, Peanut Sauce*, and very thin slices of garlic. Each guest makes rolls and dips them in the Peanut Sauce before eating.

REMARKS

The roasted rice flour (thính) should be very fine. You can buy it ready-made or prepare it yourself: roast sticky rice (nếp) in a pan over medium heat, stirring constantly until the grains are toasted inside and out. Then grind the rice in a coffee grinder to make the flour, sifting if necessary.

The manufacturing of the meatballs takes a bit of dexterity but, with a little practice, it can be accomplished in 30 minutes (especially if you cheat a little and knead each ball only 30 times!)

You can cook the meatballs in advance and reheat them in the microwave or grill just before serving.

Grilled Pork Spareribs with Honey
Sườn Nướng

This kind of marinade is found, with some variations, throughout Asia, which explains the large variety of ingredients. You can omit some of them without risk; the result will still be delicious.

❧

For a more typical and authentic Vietnamese preparation, season the ribs with fresh lemongrass (*Sườn Nướng Sả**).

Serves 4 ~ ⧗
- 2 lb pork ribs (1 rack)
- 2 tablespoons brown sugar
- ½ teaspoon pepper
- 2 tablespoons soy sauce (*xì dầu*)
- 2 tablespoons honey
- 1 tablespoon Hoisin sauce
- 1 tablespoon vinegar
- 1 tablespoon brandy
- 2 cloves garlic, crushed

1. Cut the rack of ribs into four pieces. You can also ask the butcher to saw it in half lengthwise, if you prefer pieces that are not too wide.

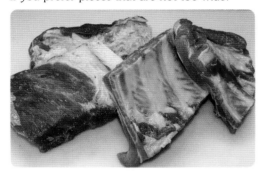

2. In a pan, heat the brown sugar with an equal amount of water. Turn off the heat as soon as the mix begins to color.

3. Prepare a marinade by adding all the other ingredients to the caramel that you just made. Macerate the ribs in it for at least 3 hours.

4. Drain the ribs and place them in a cooking dish. Cook in the oven at 400 °F for 30 to 40 minutes, until the meat is golden, turning them over once or twice.

Baste the meat with the cooking juice. Serve with rice, finely sliced cucumber and optionally some chili pepper.

REMARKS

Pork ribs go well with spices in general. You can, according to your taste, add a number of ingredients such as ginger, sesame oil, five-spice seasoning, etc.

You can prepare quail legs with the same marinade. They will brown in 20 minutes or so in a pan and make a good appetizer.

Grilled Pork Spareribs with Lemongrass
Sườn Nướng Sả

Serves 4 ~ ⧗

- 2 lb pork ribs (1 entire rack)
- 2 stalks lemongrass (sả)
- 1 scant teaspoon salt
- 1 fresh chili pepper
- ½ teaspoon sugar (optional)
- 1 tablespoon peanut oil

The full name of this dish is *"sườn nướng sả muối,"* indicating that salt *(muối)* is used instead of fish sauce. Although it is very simple to prepare, its taste and aroma are guaranteed to whet anybody's appetite.

1. Cut the rack of ribs into four pieces. You can also ask the butcher to cut it half lengthwise, if you prefer narrower ribs, which may look more refined.

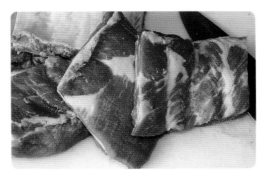

2. Remove the outer leaves and the ends of the lemongrass stalks if they are hard. Chop the lemongrass and the chili pepper as finely as possible in a food processor until they are almost reduced to a powder.

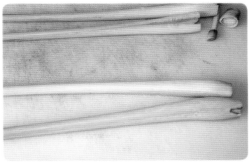

3. Combine the lemongrass, chili pepper, salt, sugar and oil. Coat the meat uniformly with the mix.

4. Place the ribs in a cooking dish, bone side up. Bake in a preheated oven at 425 °F until golden (30 to 40 minutes), turning the ribs half way through.

Baste the meat with its juice. Serve with rice, finely sliced cucumber, and possibly some chili pepper.

REMARK

Although in Vietnam, lemongrass dishes are traditionally seasoned with salt, if you want, you can replace the salt with 2 generous tablespoons of pure fish sauce.

Pork in Caramel Sauce

Thịt Kho

Serves 6 ~ ⏳ ⏳

- 2 lb lean pork belly
- Sugar
- Salt
- Pepper
- 6 eggs (optional), hard-boiled
- Pure fish sauce (*nước mắm*)

This sweet and salty simmered pork is a popular everyday food, also well known in the West. A Vietnamese family meal will almost always include some *thịt kho,* a soup, a steamed or pickled vegetable, and rice.

In a Southern variation, the water for the caramel is replaced with fresh coconut juice (but not coconut milk, which would make the sauce too greasy).

1. Cut the pork into 1.5-inch cubes, leaving the rind on.

2. In a pot, make a caramel by heating 3 heaping tablespoons of sugar with ½ tablespoon of water. The result should be golden brown, not black. When the caramel is ready, add a cup of water, 2 teaspoons of salt, and a generous tablespoon of sugar.

3. Place the pork belly cubes in a single layer at the bottom of the caramel pot, packing them next to one another, making sure they are all immersed. Bring the pot to a strong boil, skimming the impurities at the surface, for 2 or 3 minutes. Lower the heat until the liquid is barely boiling, but boiling nonetheless. Cover tightly. Simmer for at least 1 hour until the meat becomes tender. (Test by sticking a fork into it.)

4. Optionally, peel the hard-boiled eggs. Add to the pot, increase the heat, and cook for another 30 minutes. Taste and adjust the seasoning with fish sauce. Increase the heat some more to reduce the juice and color the meat.

Serve with rice. You can accompany it with slices of cucumber, Pickled Bean Sprouts (*Dua Giá*)*, or pickled mustard greens (*dua cải*); the bitterness of the mustard greens nicely offsets the saltiness of this dish.

REMARKS

The secret to success is raising the heat at the end of the cooking time: this allows the sauce to thicken and lends the meat an appetizing color.

Add fish sauce only at the end in order to limit the odor. Open the windows anyway, but mind the neighbors!

You will generally find leaner cuts of pork belly in Asian supermarkets.

Shrimp Wrapped in Pork
Tôm Ba Đình

This exquisite dish is a well kept secret. It was served in a little restaurant in Paris called "Ba Đình," run by Vietnamese workers, close to the École Polytechnique. Its preparation is much easier if you can get hold of a meat slicer.

Serves 8 ~ ⧗ ⧗ ⧗ ⧗

- 2 lb large shrimp (25/lb or larger)
- 2 lb thick pork belly, not too lean
- 5 tablespoons pure fish sauce (*nước mắm*)
- 1 teaspoon pepper
- 1 teaspoon sugar
- 1 large shallot

Serve with:

- Scallion Oil (*Mỡ Hành Lá*)*
- Angel hair (rice vermicelli, *bánh hỏi*), fresh or frozen
- Aromatic Herb Platter (*Diã Rau Sống*)*
- *Nước Mắm* Dip (*Nước Mắm Pha*)*

1. Place the meat in the freezer to let it harden a bit without freezing completely: it will be much easier to cut. This can take 45 minutes or more, depending on the freezer temperature. Cut into strips, the thinnest possible. Each piece should be wide enough to wrap a shrimp.

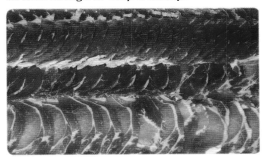

2. Combine the fish sauce, sugar, pepper, and finely chopped shallot. Pour this sauce on the meat without disturbing the slices. If you have time, allow them to marinate for a few hours (this is not indispensable, since the slices of meat should be very thin).

3. Wrap a piece of meat around each shrimp: the shrimp should be fully covered. Press the meat so that it sticks well, and the shape of the shrimp shows through.

4. Grill over high heat just before eating (about 5 minutes on each side) on charcoal if possible; if not, on an electric grill, but above all, not in the oven! Remove as soon as the meat is cooked. The shrimp cook very fast and may harden.

Baste with a little Scallion Oil*. Serve with angel hair, also garnished with Scallion Oil, a large platter of fresh herbs, and *Nước Mắm* Dip*.

REMARKS

The meat should be neither too fat nor too lean: pork fillet, for example, is too lean.

If the shrimp are not completely thawed, plunge the sealed bag into warm water for a few minutes.

Do not season the shrimp. It is preferable to wrap them at the latest possible moment, because if they don't marinate, they will stay crunchier.

Place the wrapped shrimp side by side, close to one another, so that the meat wrap doesn't undo itself. If you chill them in the refrigerator before cooking, the meat will stay on even better.

You can prepare this dish ahead of time and reheat it on a grill or in a microwave oven. To keep the shrimp moist, baste them with Scallion Oil* before reheating.

If you don't have angel hair, Rice Noodles (*Bún*)* can be substituted.

Stir-Fried Shrimp with Cashews
Tôm Rang Hột Điều

Serves 8 ~ ⏳

- 2 lb large shrimp
- 1 small garlic clove
- ½ teaspoon pepper
- 1 tablespoon wheat flour
- 3 or 4 tablespoons peanut oil
- 3 or 4 large scallions (*hành lá*)
- 8 oz cashews

This dish is an adaptation of the traditional *Tôm Rang Muối**. It is quick, easy to make, and suitable for all occasions, large or small.

1. Shell and devein the shrimp. Wash and dry them very thoroughly.

2. Peel and crush the garlic. Mix it well with the pepper, then combine with the shrimp.

3. Powder with flour, but not too much; these are not fritters!

4. In a pan, heat the oil over very high heat. Place a single layer of shrimp in the pan. Stir very quickly. Remove as soon as the shrimp are a bit crispy and lightly browned. Repeat the operation until all are cooked, and place them on a serving platter.

5. Cut the white parts of the scallions into ⅛-inch pieces. Toss them, along with the cashews, into the same pan that was used for cooking the shrimp. Season with salt. Sauté for several minutes until the cashews are browned. Pour onto the shrimp.

Serve very hot, as an appetizer or as a main course with rice. You can garnish it with some moderately hot chili pepper slices.

REMARKS

Choose shrimp larger than those you would use for *Tôm Rang Muối**. If possible, buy Asian prawns.

You can use raw or roasted cashews.

Dry-Braised Shrimp

Tôm Rim

Historically, this simple dish was commonly made in the countryside using freshwater shrimp. Since it remained nevertheless fairly expensive, in poorer or stricter families, children were sometimes served a bowl of rice with only a couple of shrimp on top.

You need to select shrimp with very thin shells, as they are cooked and eaten with the shell on.

The most usual Vietnamese cooking methods can be classified as follows:

- *Kho:* simmered in liquid
- *Ram* (for meat) or *rim* (for shrimp): similar to *kho,* but in a dryer environment
- *Xào:* sautéed
- *Rang:* between sautéed and fried; less oil than for frying, higher heat that sautéing
- *Chiên:* fried

Serves 4 ~ ⧗

- 1 lb very thin-shelled shrimp (the size of a little finger)
- 2 cloves garlic
- 3 tablespoons peanut oil
- 1 scant teaspoon sugar
- ½ teaspoon salt
- 1 pinch of pepper
- 1 tablespoon pure fish sauce (*nước mắm*)
- A few scallions (*hành lá*, optional)

1. Wash the shrimp well and dry them on a paper towel. Don't shell them, but remove the heads and the legs.

2. Crush the garlic and sauté it in the oil.

3. Turn the heat all the way up, and add the shrimp, sugar, salt, and pepper. Stir well, keeping the heat high so that the shrimp don't produce liquid.

4. When the shrimp are opaque, turn off the heat, add the fish sauce, and mix. Season to taste.

It is imperative that this dish be eaten with Steamed Rice*. It should therefore be lightly salted, but less so than *Cá Kho**, for example. It should also be *slightly* sweet. Thus, in the end, it shouldn't be too salty, too sweet, or too bland...

REMARK

An innovation: while the shrimp are cooking, add the white ends of scallions cut into 1-inch pieces.

Vegetables and Starches

Zucchini Blossom Fritters
Bông Bí Lăn Bột Chiên

These fritters are not exclusively Vietnamese, but they are always a success. You don't need to limit yourself to zucchini blossoms, you can make fritters with all sorts of vegetables: zucchini, eggplant, carrot, broccoli, onion, and even fresh corn. In Vietnam, sweet potato is also frequently used. Shrimp fritters are prepared in the same manner.

Serves 6 ~ ⧖ ⧖

- Zucchini blossoms or other vegetables
- 10 tablespoons wheat flour
- 1 tablespoon potato starch
- 2 teaspoons baking powder
- Water
- Peanut oil

Corn fritters

1. Combine the flour, starch, and baking powder. Add water slowly while mixing until you get a somewhat liquid batter. It should pour slowly from the spoon without breaking up. Whip the batter a long time, until it is quite smooth. Let stand at least ½ hour in the refrigerator.

2. Wash and cut the vegetables. Dry them carefully. If you use corn, cut it off the cob with a knife. You will need 5 or 6 ears of corn for 10 tablespoons of flour.

3. Coat the pieces of vegetable by plunging them into the batter (for corn, simply combine corn kernels with the batter). Fry them, making sure there is enough oil to completely submerge each piece.

4. Drain on absorbent paper, sprinkle with salt, and serve immediately.

REMARKS

You can use the same batter for Banana Fritters* or shrimp fritters.

Once cooked, the fritters should be light and crispy. If they are hard, the batter was too thick. If they spread in the oil, the batter was too liquid.

The potato starch helps make the fritters crunchy. It is best not to put salt in the batter, as it will make the oil pop and splatter.

Roasted Eggplant
Cà Tím Dầm Nước Mắm

This simple, yet tasty dish is a very widespread method for serving eggplant in Vietnam.

The regular Western eggplant works well, but whenever possible, we prefer the Asian variety, which has a more gentle, subtle taste. In the store, it is easily recognizable by its lighter color and elongated shape. Unlike Western eggplants, it is never bitter and you don't have to peel or disgorge it before cooking.

Figure one Asian eggplant per person or one Western eggplant for two people.

Another common way to prepare eggplant is to sauté it with minced onion and perilla leaves *(tía tô)*.

Serves 6 ~ ⧗

- 6 small Asian eggplants
- 1 cup Scallion Oil (*Mỡ Hành Lá*)*
- 1 cup *Nước Mắm* Dip (*Nước Mắm Pha*)*

1. Poke holes all over the outside of the eggplants so they won't explode while cooking. Cook either in the microwave (8 minutes for two eggplants) or in a regular oven (15 to 30 minutes at 400 °F). Check that they are well done; the flesh should be very soft to the touch.

2. Pass the eggplants under running cold water, so the skin will detach easily from the flesh. Peel and split lengthwise. Arrange on a serving platter.

3. Cover with *Nước Mắm* Dip* and Scallion Oil*. Serve immediately, accompanied by rice and a meat dish.

REMARKS

Cooking in the conventional oven takes longer, but yields a better flavor. Better still, grill them over a charcoal fire.

Pour the Scallion Oil* and *Nước Mắm* Dip* over the eggplants while they are still piping hot; by allowing them to soak-up the seasoning, this will infuse them with flavor.

You can replace the Scallion Oil* with minced shallots or onions fried in oil. Once they are browned, remove them immediately from the heat so they don't burn. The scallion has a more delicate taste; shallots have a stronger flavor, while being crunchier than onions.

You can cut the eggplants into smaller pieces before serving. This makes them easier to eat, but less pleasing to the eye.

Green Vegetables
Cải Xào, Cải Hấp

Vietnamese people consume a lot of vegetables. Those are present at every meal, often boiled or steamed, seasoned with fish sauce or soy sauce. A normal meal in an average family will likely consist of rice, clear soup *(canh)*, vegetables, and meat.

The word "cải" means "leafy vegetable," and there is a large variety of these *(cải bẹ xanh, cải bẹ trắng, cải làn, cải rổ, cải ná,* etc.), which can be eaten in diverse ways: sautéed *(xào),* boiled *(luộc)* or steamed *(hấp),* in soups, or in salads.

Serves 4 ~ ⧖

- Green leafy vegetables
- 2 cloves garlic or 1 small onion
- Peanut oil
- Sesame oil
- Soy sauce or pure fish sauce *(nước mắm)*

Soak and wash the vegetables one type at a time (usually, different kinds of vegetables are not mixed).

Sautéed:

- Cut into 1-inch lengths.

- In the peanut oil, sauté ¼ onion or 1 garlic clove. (One or the other, not both!)

- Add the vegetables and sauté.

- Season with salt (or pure fish sauce) and some pepper.

Boiled or steamed:

- Cook rapidly in boiling water or steam. Test by pinching a stalk. Drain well.

- Season with 1 tablespoon peanut oil and ½ teaspoon sesame oil. Add soy sauce to taste.

Sauce:

You can serve the boiled or steamed vegetables "as is." They will be dipped in *Thịt Kho** or *Cá Kho** juice. You can just as easily serve them with this simple sauce:

- Quarter two hard-boiled eggs. Crush the yolks with a fork.

- Add ¼ cup of pure fish sauce and mix.

REMARKS

Don't cook the vegetables for too long. Vietnamese people like to keep them on the crunchy side.

If you season with fish sauce, use pure fish sauce, never *nước mắm* dip.

In the same fashion, you can prepare:

- Chrysanthemum leaves *(rau tần ô)*

- Chinese chives *(hẹ)*

- Kale, mustard greens, or any leafy green

As the national vegetable, water spinach deserves a special mention (see *Rau Muống Xào Tỏi**).

Fried Rice

Cơm Chiên

Serves 4

- 2 cups cold cooked rice
- 2 Chinese sausages (*lạp xưởng*)
- 1 small onion
- 2 slices of cooked ham (optional)
- ½ clove garlic
- 2 tablespoons peanut oil
- Salt and pepper
- A few scallions (*hành lá*, optional)
- ½ cup cooked peas (optional)

This is a leftover dish that is actually better when prepared with cold rice from the day before. The rice grains need to be separate, yet tender.

1. Separate the rice grains with your fingers (it's easier to do while the rice is still warm).

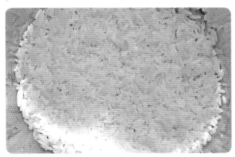

2. Slice the Chinese sausages, cut the ham into little squares, and dice the onion into tiny pieces.

3. Heat the oil in a pan and sauté the onion and garlic. Add the sausage slices, the ham, and the rice. Stir, mix, and let it cook.

Season with salt and pepper. Add the peas and the chopped scallion, stir, and turn off the heat. Everyone can add pepper to their taste.

4. The cooking takes about 15 minutes. At the end, the grains of rice should be separate and a little shiny from the oil.

REMARK

It is common to garnish the top with a very thin omelet, rolled up and cut into thin strips (1/16 inch thick).

Pickled Vegetables
Đồ Chua

For a 1-quart jar ~ ⧗ ⧗

- Carrots
- Cauliflower
- Tender celery stalks without the leaves
- Daikon radishes (*củ cải*), as fat as or fatter than a carrot
- Young ginger (*gừng*, optional)
- 1 cup white vinegar
- ¾ cup sugar
- 2 cups water
- 1 tablespoon salt

These little pickles are present at all the meals. You can snack on them between courses, or eat them as an accompaniment to the main dishes.

❧

In general, turnip and carrots are used. Very fine green beans can also be added. This preparation keeps in a refrigerator for several months, up to a year even.

1. Wash the vegetables. Cut them into little decorative pieces:
   - ginger: very thin slices
   - celery: diagonal ½-inch-wide pieces
   - carrots and turnips: ¹⁄₁₆-inch-thick slices or sticks
   - other vegetables: bite-sized pieces

2. Bring a pot of salted water to a boil. Blanch the vegetables for 15 seconds. Drain and let cool.

3. Combine vinegar, sugar, water, and salt. Boil and let cool.

4. Pack as many vegetables as possible at the bottom of a jar and pour the vinegar preparation on top.

Let cool, and then put the lid on. Wait at least two days before eating.

REMARKS

The use of ginger is not traditional, but it is a tasty innovation! You can also try shallots. They are a bit strong, but not unpleasant.

Curiously, blanching the vegetables causes them to stay crunchy. This also prevents mold.

Garlic can also be prepared the same way.

Sautéed Wheat Noodles
Mì Xào

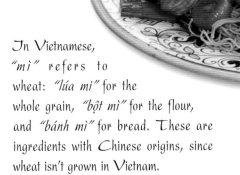

In Vietnamese, *"mì"* refers to wheat: *"lúa mi"* for the whole grain, *"bột mì"* for the flour, and *"bánh mì"* for bread. These are ingredients with Chinese origins, since wheat isn't grown in Vietnam.

Mì xào, however, is very widespread there. It is served with all sorts of garnishes: beef, pork, or shellfish. The noodles can be fried *(mì xào dòn)* or boiled *(mì xào mềm).*

Serves 10 ~ ⧗ ⧗ ⧗

- Chinese wheat noodles (*mì*), 3 to 4 oz per person
- Soy sauce (*xì dầu*)
- Oyster sauce (*dầu hào*)
- Peanut oil
- 1 tablespoon tapioca starch (*bột mì tinh*)
- 1 shallot

Vegetables:

- 1 handful snow peas
- 1 carrot
- 1 small broccoli head
- 1 bamboo shoot
- A few sprigs of Chinese chives (*hẹ*, optional)

Meat, choice of:

- 1 lb beef, the most tender possible, sliced very thinly
- or 1 lb pork loin or shoulder, cut into thin slices
- or shellfish (shrimp, small squid, scallops)

1. If using beef, prepare as in Sautéed Beef with Onions*; in particular, sprinkle on a bit of flour before cooking and season with soy sauce instead of fish sauce.

   In a large pan, sauté a thinly sliced shallot in oil. Add the meat or fish and cook (very quickly in the case of beef, until fully cooked for pork and shellfish). Remove the meat and leave the cooking juices in the pan.

2. Wash the vegetables. Only use the lower end of the Chinese chive (white end), cut into 1-inch pieces. Cut the other vegetables into small bite-sized morsels.

3. Pour a little oil into the pan with the meat juices, then add all the vegetables (except for the Chinese chives). Add the snow peas last, as they cook quickly. Adjust the seasoning to your taste with soy sauce and oyster sauce (1 tablespoon is generally enough). Add water if needed, so as to make a sauce. At the end, dilute 1 tablespoon of tapioca starch, add to the pan, and stir. The sauce should be a bit thick.

4. To keep the vegetables crunchy, don't let them cook for too long. After turning off the heat, add the Chinese chives. Mix the vegetables and meat: the garnish is ready.

5. Prepare the noodles. Choose:

   - Either **Mì Xào Dòn:** rapidly blanch the noodles by plunging them into boiling water (around 10 seconds, follow the instructions on the package). Let them drain, then dry for an hour. Make individual "nests" (2 per person) by rolling them around your fingers. Plunge them into boiling oil until they are browned. Remove and drain.

   - Or **Mì Xào Mềm:** fully cook the noodles in boiling water.

Place the noodles on a serving platter and put the garnish on top. Pour the sauce over the meat and vegetables and pepper with a few turns from the grinder.

Serve immediately.

REMARK

So that the *Mì Xào Dòn* stays crunchy, fry the noodles only after everything else is ready. Add the garnish and sauce at the last minute, just before serving.

Sautéed Bean Threads
Miến Xào

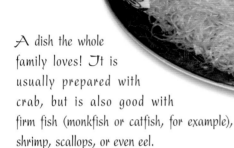

A dish the whole family loves! It is usually prepared with crab, but is also good with firm fish (monkfish or catfish, for example), shrimp, scallops, or even eel.

෴

Contrary to appearances, *miến* is not made with a classic flour, but with mung bean flour. Don't confuse it with rice noodles (*bún*).

Serves 5 ~ ⌛ ⌛

- 1 lb mung bean thread (*miến*)
- 1 lb crab or 1½ lb firm fish
- 3 minced shallots
- 3 scallions (*hành lá*), cut into 1-inch pieces
- Peanut oil
- Pure fish sauce (*nước mắm*)
- Pepper

1. Soak the bean thread in hot water 3 or 4 hours ahead of time, then drain.

2. If using crab, shred it and discard the small cartilage ribbons. If using fish, cut into bite-sized pieces. For eel, skin it first, then sauté it and remove the backbone.

3. Fry the chopped shallots in 2 tablespoons of oil. Turn up the heat, add the crab or fish, and sauté. Season with pure fish sauce, pepper, and a few of the scallions. Transfer this preparation to another container, leaving the juice in the pan.

4. Add some oil to the pan and sauté the bean thread for 10 minutes, stirring continuously. Season with fish sauce (about ½ tablespoon) and pepper to taste.

Place the bean thread on a serving plate and arrange the crab preparation on top. Decorate with the remaining scallions. Each guest adds pepper to taste and possibly pure fish sauce.

REMARKS

If you prefer a less pronounced taste, season the crab with salt instead of fish sauce.

If the crab produces enough juice, you can skip the oil when sautéing the bean thread. The result may be lighter, but it sure tastes better with a lot of oil! If you use fish, the heat should be very high, as the fish will produce a lot of liquid.

To reveal the whole flavor of this dish, it is important to add pepper before eating.

Mushrooms Stuffed with Shrimp
Nấm Nhồi Tôm

As you may have guessed from the ingredients, this a Chinese-Vietnamese treat. The traditional Vietnamese version is similar, minus the sauce. However, since the sauce brings an obvious flavor benefit, we chose to depart from tradition for once.

This refined dish is a bit expensive, and its preparation is relatively elaborate. For an appetizer, choose small mushrooms, as they are more elegant. For a main course, you can pick larger ones.

Serves 4 ~ ⧗ ⧗ ⧗ ⧗

- 16 shiitake mushrooms (*nấm hương*) dried or fresh, medium sized (2 inches in diameter)
- 1 tablespoon tapioca starch (*bột mì tinh*) or potato starch

Stuffing:

- 10 oz medium-sized shrimp
- ½ egg white
- ½ teaspoon salt
- ¼ teaspoon pepper

Sauce:

- 1 tablespoon oil
- 1 tablespoon white wine
- 1 teaspoon tapioca starch (*bột mì tinh*)
- ½ cup Chicken Stock (*Nước Lèo*)* or 1 teaspoon mushroom powder
- 1 tablespoon oyster sauce (*dầu hào*)
- 1 teaspoon sesame oil (*dầu mè*)

Faux Crab Eggs:

- 1 egg
- 6 drops red food coloring

1. If using dried shiitake mushrooms, soak them for at least 3 hours (or overnight if possible). Drain them well, squeezing slightly. Cut and discard the stems.

2. Peel the shrimp and run them in the food processor together with the other stuffing ingredients. Process for a long time, and then work it some more with a large spoon to get a compact mixture.

3. After coating your hands with oil, form the stuffing into balls. Coat the inside edge of each mushroom with tapioca starch (so that it will be sticky) and press a stuffing ball onto the mushroom.

4. Steam for 10 minutes (and no more, as the shrimp shouldn't be overcooked).

5. **Sauce:** Gently heat some oil in a frying pan, then turn off the heat. Add the white wine and tapioca starch. Turn the heat back on and add the broth (or the mushroom powder diluted in ½ cup of water). As soon as the sauce boils, add the oyster sauce. Remove from heat and add the sesame oil (which should not cook).

6. **Faux Crab Eggs (Gạch Cua Giả):** Beat an egg for a long time so as to introduce air bubbles, then add 6 drops of red food coloring. Cook for 10 minutes in a large double boiler: the egg will expand. Let it cool completely, then chop it with a knife. This preparation keeps a long time.

Just before serving, pour the sauce over the mushrooms. Decorate by sprinkling with Faux Crab Eggs and place a cilantro leaf on top of each mushroom.

Serve by itself as a snack or as a main course with rice.

REMARK

Unlike *Chạo Tôm**, which also consists of ground shrimp, this dish doesn't require large shrimp.

Sautéed Water Spinach with Garlic
Rau Muống Xào Tỏi

Rau muống was once a humble vegetable: only people from North Vietnam would eat it, and it was disdained in the South. They would even say of a Northerner that had settled in the South: "He can talk with a Southern accent all he wants, but after three words the stalk of *rau muống* sticks out of his mouth!" However, in recent decades, the inhabitants of the South have also adopted *rau muống,* which has become a truly national vegetable, highly prized by all levels of society.

Although in the South it is thrown out, the cooking water is very popular in the North, where it is made into a broth. The common wisdom has it that a bowl of this equals a bowl of vitamins.

We are presenting here the most current way of cooking *rau muống.* However, it is also consumed simply boiled and dipped in *tương bắc.*

Serves 4 ~ ⏳
- 1 bunch water spinach (*rau muống*)
- 2 tablespoons peanut oil
- 2 cloves garlic

1. Wash the water spinach. Separate the leaves from the stalks. Break the stalks into 2-inch-long pieces. If necessary, discard the ends that are too old and too hard: this is the case when you feel resistance under your fingers when breaking the stalk.

2. Blanch the stalks and leaves for 1 minute in boiling water with a pinch of salt. Drain well.

3. Heat the oil in a frying pan. Add the crushed garlic (without browning it) and the water spinach, seasoning lightly with salt. Cook over medium heat for 5 minutes if eating it Vietnamese style (or 10 minutes if you don't like crunchy vegetables).

Sautéed water spinach is eaten with pure fish sauce or *Nước Mắm* Dip*. Fermented bean sauce (*tương bắc*) is usually reserved for steamed or boiled water spinach.

REMARKS

Water spinach spoils fast. It's best to wash it as soon as possible.

To keep the leaves a pretty green color, be sure to add a little salt to the water before blanching.

Water Spinach Broth: After removing the cooked vegetables, add a quartered tomato (in Vietnam, *quả sấu*, a fruit from the South, is also used) and a few drops of lime juice.

Sautéed Mixed Vegetables
Rau Xào Thập Cẩm

The idea here is to sauté together many different vegetables (*"thập"* means 10 in Sino-Vietnamese). Although the vegetables found abroad vary and obviously won't be the same as in Vietnam, you will always include bean sprouts, wood ear mushrooms, and two or three other types of mushrooms. In Vietnam, people often use celery heart and bamboo shoots.

Serves 4 ~ ⧗ ⧗

- ½ onion
- 3 tablespoon peanut oil
- 1 teaspoon mushroom seasoning (optional)

Choice of:

- Straw mushrooms (*nấm rơm*), fresh or canned
- Mung bean sprouts (*giá*)
- Wood ear mushrooms (*nấm mèo*)
- Shiitake mushrooms (*nấm hương*)
- Firm tofu (*tầu hủ*)
- Celery hearts
- Bamboo shoots (*măng*)
- Turnips
- Chinese chives (*hẹ*), white parts only
- Bok choy (*cải bẹ trắng*)
- Baby corn

1. If using dried mushrooms, soak them overnight. Drain them and discard the stems if hard.

2. Wash and cut the vegetables:
   - Chinese chive: 2-inch pieces
   - baby corn: split in two
   - wood ear mushrooms: bite-sized pieces
   - bamboo shoots: sliced
   - tofu: 1 x ½ x ½ inch pieces
   - turnip: sliced
   - celery: sliced or cut diagonally
   - other vegetables: bite-sized pieces

3. Sauté the minced onion in oil. Add the vegetables that take the longest to cook (wood ear mushroom, turnips), and then add the rest. Allow to cook for about 15 minutes, according to taste. Add the bean sprouts and the Chinese chives only at the end, just before turning off the heat.

Season with salt and pepper or soy sauce. Optionally, add the mushroom seasoning diluted in water. Mix well and turn off the heat immediately.

Fried Tofu

Tầu Hủ Chiên

This is
a simple,
common dish for
a family meal. You need
to buy tofu that is more compact and firm
than regular tofu. It is usually sold in the form
of small loaves.

The *tương bắc* for dipping is sold in a bottle.
As its name indicates, it is a product from the
North ("*bắc*" means "north"). It is widely
available: the most famous is *tương bắc cự đà*.

Serves 4 ~ ⏳

- ½ lb firm tofu (*tầu hủ*)
- Peanut oil

For dipping:

- Fermented bean sauce
  (*tương bắc*)

Hanoï. Petit Lac.

1. Cut the tofu into 1 x 1 x ½ inch pieces.

2. Heat the oil in a large pan. Arrange the tofu pieces in the pan in a single layer.

3. Fry, turning the tofu from time to time. Before removing the pieces, wait until they have expanded and are a bit hard on the outside; otherwise they will deflate. This can take up to 20 minutes

Drain on a paper towel. Serve immediately with the fermented bean sauce (*tương bắc*) in little individual bowls. Eat very hot.

REMARK

If you can't find *tương bắc*, you can use *nước mắm* or soy sauce for dipping. (But of course, don't expect it to taste as good.)

Steamed Sticky Rice
Xôi Đậu Xanh

The word *"xôi"* means "steamed rice." Here, to be more precise, we are talking about *xôi nếp,* which is prepared with sticky rice, *gạo nếp.*

❧

There are many variants of *xôi nếp:* the most ordinary type can replace steamed white rice with some dishes, or it can be sweetened with coconut for breakfast or dessert.

❧

The version presented here is a little elaborate, the rice grains being coated with mung bean paste. In South Vietnam, this is traditionally served with *chè* or *cơm rượu.*

Serves 6 ~ ⏳ ⏳

- ½ lb sticky rice (*gạo nếp*)
- ¼ lb peeled mung beans (*đậu xanh*)
- 1 pinch of salt
- 3 tablespoons peanut oil

1. Soak the sticky rice and beans separately for 3 to 4 hours.

2. Steam the beans or cook them in a pot with very little water so that, after cooking, the beans are still separate, and not a mush. Add the salt. Make a fine paste by crushing the beans with a spoon. Let cool.

3. Drain the raw rice well. Mix it carefully with the bean paste, making sure you don't leave lumps.

4. Steam the mix over medium heat: use a steamer with small regular holes and spread the rice in a thin layer (⅓ inch). If the holes are too big, place a piece of cheesecloth underneath. The rice cooks very quickly.

After 5 minutes, stir and separate the grains with a fork. Sprinkle the oil all over. Mix well, or the rice will become hard when cooled. Taste and turn off the heat as soon as the rice is tender. You need to make sure that the rice is not too wet at the end of the cooking.

Pour the cooked rice onto a large plate. Let it cool and separate the rice some more with a fork. For the *xôi* to be a success, the grains should be completely detached from each other and very tender.

This *xôi* is most often eaten as a sweet dish: each guest adds sugar to taste in their bowl.

REMARKS

Perfectionists remove the rice from the steamer when it is almost cooked, coat it again with bean paste by shaking it in a large jar, and steam it some more. This *Xôi* used to be a dessert. However, as it is a little more refined, the Vietnamese overseas have gotten in the habit of serving it in place of simple *xôi nếp*, with fried and sliced Chinese sausages (*lạp xưởng*), sliced pork roll (*chả lụa*), or pork skewers.

Soups

Crab Noodle Soup
Bánh Canh Cua

The soup shown here is a bit elaborate, and more "noble" than *phở* or *hủ tiếu*, for instance, because crab and fish are expensive. Prized in the South, it is also found in Central Vietnam, with the difference that the broth is slightly thickened with flour. Since this is a refined soup, serve it in small quantities only, at the end of a meal.

Serves 6 ~ ⌛ ⌛

- 6 cups Chicken Stock (*Nước Lèo*)*
- 1 ½ lb fresh translucent noodles (*bánh canh*)
- 6 scallions (*hành lá*)
- 12 sprigs cilantro (*ngò*)
- Pure fish sauce (*nước mắm*)
- Pepper

Garnish:

- 1 small raw ham hock (optional)
- 1 or 2 shallots
- ½ lb crab meat
- Peanut oil
- Salt, pepper

The name *"bánh canh"* designates the thick translucent noodles that are the base for the soup, as well as the soup itself.

The soup was previously reserved for breakfast or snacks and, like many other dishes, was available only from street vendors.

1. Prepare the Chicken Stock*: for taste, a hen is actually better than a regular chicken. Once cooked the hen has no further use in this recipe, but can be used in other dishes, such as Banana Blossom Salad (*Gỏi Bắp Chuối*)*. Filter the stock, add salt to taste, and set aside.

2. If a ham hock is used, put it whole in boiling water and leave it until barely cooked (tender but not too soft). Cut it in $1/16$ x 1 x 1 inch strips, leaving the skin on. Sauté a minced shallot in two tablespoons of oil. Add the ham strips and continue to cook for 1 more minute.

3. Shred the crab meat and discard the transparent ribbon-like cartilage. Sauté a minced shallot in 2 tablespoons of oil, add the crab, mix, and sauté for 30 seconds. Season with salt and pepper to taste.

4. Cut the translucent noodles into 2-inch-long pieces. Just before serving, place them for a few minutes in the boiling stock until soft.

Serve in individual bowls: First, place a small handful of noodles at the bottom, then pour in the stock. Finally, top with a little garnish of crab and, optionally, a few slices of cooked ham hock. Decorate with cilantro leaves and chopped scallions. Serve immediately.

Each guest seasons to taste with a bit of pepper and pure fish sauce.

Bánh Canh Cá Giò Heo (Noodle Soup with Ham Hock and Fish, the most common variant of this dish): slice a fillet of good fish, such as monkfish or large sole, into thin pieces; sauté in oil with minced shallot. Use this garnish to prepare the soup as above.

REMARK

If there is crab juice, pour it into the stock. And if the stock is tasty, pour a lot of it into each bowl! An unconventional, yet nice, touch: garnish the top of the soup with a few fried shallots.

Clear Soup with Fish Balls
Canh Cá Thác Lác

A Vietnamese family meal always includes a clear soup *(canh)*. This can be as simple as a clear broth with a little fish sauce and a few vegetables, or a very elaborate soup with crab, meat, or fish, and again vegetables.

Cá thác lác is an amazing fish. Once kneaded, its flesh rapidly takes on an elasticity that perfectly imitates pork roll *(giò lụa)*. You can use it to make balls for this pretty soup. Since it is light, people are always willing to have a bowl of it after a large meal.

Serves 6 ~ ⧗

- ½ lb frozen notopterus *(cá thác lác)*
- 2 tablespoons pure fish sauce *(nước mắm)*
- ¼ teaspoon white pepper
- 1-inch-long piece of ginger *(gừng)*
- 6 large leaves Chinese mustard *(cải bẹ xanh)*
- 3 scallions *(hành lá)*

Chinese mustard *(cải bẹ xanh)* goes perfectly with fish. Its strong taste adds dimension and personality to this simple soup.

1. Allow the fish to thaw slowly overnight in the refrigerator (and not in hot water).

2. In a large bowl, combine the fish, fish sauce, and pepper. Then, with the help of a large metal spoon, "knead" it: scrape while pressing the surface of the fish with the back of the spoon, as if trying to smooth it, until you get a uniform and springy consistency (10 minutes at most, otherwise the "dough" becomes too rubbery).

3. Wash the mustard leaves and cut into 1-inch-wide pieces. Wash and chop the scallions. Peel the ginger and cut it into slices.

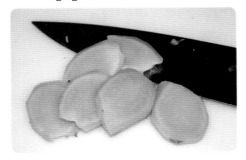

4. In a pot, bring 1 qt of water to a boil with the ginger

5. Using a teaspoon dipped in oil, drop bite-sized pieces of fish dough into the boiling water (the pieces need not be round or regular). Leave them 1 or 2 minutes. When they float to the surface, they are cooked.

6. Toss the Chinese mustard into the pot, starting with the thicker pieces that take longer to cook. After about a minute, add the chopped scallions and turn off the heat. The broth will be very clear.

Season to taste with fish sauce or salt. Salt works best, as fish sauce is a little too strong for this delicate soup. Serve in a large common bowl, or, if you are in a fancy mood, individual ones.

REMARKS

You need to have the vegetables ready before cooking the fish. If you don't, the fish might cook for too long and lose its flavor. Don't cook the mustard too much, either: Vietnamese people like their vegetables very crunchy.

Variant: Replace the mustard with a tomato cut into six pieces and a few stalks of Vietnamese dill (*thìa là*) cut into 2-inch-long pieces. Turn off the heat immediately.

Sour Soup with Fish
Canh Chua

This soup is normally prepared with *cá lóc,* but you can use just about any fish, as long as it doesn't taste too strong and is not too fatty (therefore, avoid salmon).

You can also prepare *canh chua* with pineapple instead of vegetables, but don't combine the two recipes! With pineapple, choose even leaner fish, such as red snapper or monkfish.

A controversial culinary trend in South Vietnam in recent decades is to add sugar everywhere, resulting in a sweet and sour soup. In fact, *canh chua* is not sweet, except, of course, when it contains pineapple.

Serves 6 ~ ⏳ ⏳

- 1 medium *cá lóc* (1 lb), or monkfish, catfish, tilapia...
- 1 tablespoon pitted tamarind (*me*)
- Pure fish sauce (*nước mắm*)
- Salt, pepper
- Chili pepper

Vegetable soup:

- 1 ripe tomato
- 6 or 8 okras (*đậu bắp*)
- 2 taro stalks (*bạc hà*)
- 1 handful mung bean sprouts (*gía*)
- 1 bunch saw-leaf herb or culantro (*ngò gai*, important!)

Pineapple soup:

- 1 fresh pineapple
- 6 stalks rice paddy herb (*ngò om*)

1. Dissolve the tamarind in a glass of boiling water. Strain the liquid thus obtained, to avoid clouding the broth with tamarind particles.

2. Wash and prepare the vegetables:
   - Cut the tomato into 6 sections.
   - Cut the okras diagonally in half.
   - Cut the taro stalks diagonally in ½-inch-wide pieces.
   - Or, if using pineapple, cut it into sticks the size of a little finger.

3. Clean the fish, taking care to remove the hard fins.

4. In a pot, combine about 1 qt of water (not too much water, but enough to cover the fish) with the tamarind juice and a little salt and pepper. Depending on the size of the fish, boil it whole or in slices for about 10 minutes, then carefully remove it from the broth.

5. Add the tomato and okras to the broth. Wait 2 minutes, and then add the taro stalks and the mung bean sprouts. Turn off the heat immediately. If you are using pineapple, cook it for 5 minutes in the broth instead of the vegetables. Season with fish sauce and pepper, tasting and adjusting the seasoning.

6. Chop the herbs finely (*ngò gai* or *ngò om*).

Pour the soup into a large bowl. Place the pieces of fish on top, then garnish with the chopped herbs. Decorate with large red chili peppers, split or sliced.

If the fish is whole, serve it separately, accompanied with little bowls of pure fish sauce, possibly spiced up with slices of chili peppers.

REMARKS

Cá lóc is sold frozen. *Cá bông lau* likewise; you may also find it in slices, which is a more convenient approach. Figure one slice per person.

It is absolutely necessary to taste the soup to ensure that it is adequately sour. If not, add tamarind. Many people also use sugar, but it is not traditional: after all, it's a sour soup, not sweet and sour!

Crab and Asparagus Soup
Canh Măng Tây Cua

Serves 6 ~ ⏳

- 6 cups Chicken Stock (*Nước Lèo*)*
- 1 ½ lb asparagus
- ½ lb crabmeat
- 1 egg
- 6 sprigs cilantro (*ngò*)
- Salt
- ½ tablespoon mushroom seasoning (optional)
- 1 tablespoon tapioca starch (*bột mì tinh*)

Here is a light soup with a delicate aroma, suitable for any honored guest! It provides an excellent refined finish to a good meal.

Literally, *"măng tây"* means "French bamboo," since asparagus, very rare in Vietnam, was planted in the highlands by the French.

The success of this soup depends entirely on the quality of the crab: if possible, use fresh crabmeat (Alaskan king crab legs for example).

The mushroom seasoning is a flavor enhancer, a substitute for monosodium glutamate.

DALAT — Grand Lycée

1. Clean the asparagus and peel off the hard exterior of the lower part. Cut into pieces 1 to 2 inches long.

2. Crumble the crabmeat and remove the transparent cartilage ribbons. If there is juice, add it to the broth.

3. Bring the broth to a boil. Throw in the asparagus and crab.

4. When the asparagus is just barely cooked (around 5 minutes) beat an egg yolk and pour it into the broth, stirring very fast so that you get strings.

5. Season with salt and possibly the mushroom seasoning. Thicken slightly by slowly adding a little tapioca starch until the desired consistency is reached.

Mushroom seasoning

6. Turn off the heat and serve immediately, sprinkling each bowl with cilantro leaves. Each guest adds pepper to taste.

REMARKS

Instead of king crab, you can use Canadian "snow crab," which can be found in some Asian markets. It comes frozen in little 1 lb blocks.

For the soup to be a success, it is imperative that the asparagus be a bit crunchy. Don't use pork broth as its flavor would overpower the other delicate ingredients.

Thicken the soup with cornstarch or potato starch. Wheat or rice flours have a tendency to become cloudy and liquefy too easily.

Rice Porridge with Fish
Cháo Cá

Here is a rather refined rice porridge *(cháo)*, which features expensive fish. If noodles *(bún or bánh hỏi)* were eaten during the meal, you can serve *cháo* at the end. On the other hand, if there was already rice with the main courses, you should, of course, avoid having a rice-based soup.

Unlike *cháo gà,* this recipe doesn't use toasted rice. This ensures that the soup will be creamy.

Serves 6 ~ ⏳⏳

• 6 cups Chicken Stock (*Nước Lèo*)*

• 1½ lb monkfish (or 1 large sole fillet)

• ⅔ cup raw rice

• 1 shallot

• 2-inch-long piece of ginger *(gừng)*

• Salt, pepper, oil

• 3 scallions *(hành lá)*

• 6 sprigs cilantro *(ngò)*

• Pure fish sauce *(nước mắm)*

1. Remove the bones from the fish and add them to the Chicken Stock*. Let boil for 20 minutes, then remove the bones.

2. Add the raw rice. Let the rice porridge cook until the grains are bursting, but not so much that they are reduced to mush.

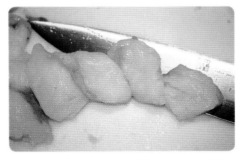

3. Cut the fish into 1-inch-thick slices, mince the shallot, and cut the ginger into very thin strands.

4. In a skillet, sauté the shallots and a heaping tablespoon of ginger in a tablespoon of oil. Over high heat, add the fish, salt, and pepper. Stop when the fish is still half raw (1 or 2 minutes) so it becomes fragrant without really cooking.

5. Add this preparation to the rice porridge, which should be very hot or even lightly boiling.

Serve in individual bowls. Sprinkle with chopped cilantro and scallions, add a turn of the pepper grinder and serve immediately. Each person seasons with pure fish sauce to taste.

REMARKS

The soup must not be too thick: if necessary, dilute it with additional broth just before serving.

You can use fish sauce for cooking and seasoning the fish, but the result may be too strong for some people's taste.

Cháo ám - in this version, all the ingredients are placed in the bottom of individual bowls:

- Fish, very thinly sliced (1/16 inch)
- Scallions, quartered lengthwise and cut into 1-inch lengths
- A pinch of ginger strands
- A teaspoon of pure fish sauce
- Some pepper

Then the boiling rice porridge is poured on top. The broth must be especially good because the fish won't produce any juice!

Rice Porridge with Chicken
Cháo Gà

This is the kind of dish that you might order in an eatery with some *gỏi,* after leaving the cinema or the "popular" theater *(cải lương* or *hát bộ).* But it can also be prepared at home to honor an unexpected guest: for that occasion, you would go out in the backyard and sacrifice one of the family chickens.

In the South, the rice is toasted before cooking. Thus, the grains will be detached and not too sticky.

Serves 6 ~ ⧗ ⧗

- ⅔ cup raw rice
  (a small handful per serving)

- 1 whole chicken

- Salt, pepper

- 2-inch-long piece of ginger *(gừng)*

- 1 tablespoon mushroom seasoning (optional)

- 3 scallions *(hành lá)*

- 6 sprigs cilantro *(ngò)*

Accompaniment:

- Banana Blossom Salad *(Gỏi Bắp Chuối)**

- *Nước Mắm* Dip *(Nước Mắm Pha)**

1. Wash and dry the rice. If it's very young rice, toast it in a skillet, stirring constantly with a wooden spoon, until it starts to turn golden (don't let it actually brown).

2. Plunge the whole chicken into a large pot of salted (1 scant tablespoon salt) and peppered (1 scant teaspoon pepper) boiling water with a few slices of peeled ginger. Cover. Remove the chicken when it is fully cooked (½ hour to 1 hour).

3. Let the chicken cool, then detach the meat by hand and put the carcass back in the pot to boil. Keep the meat for Banana Blossom Salad* or Cabbage Salad (see below).

4. When the broth is strong enough, remove the carcass and skim the surface of the broth to remove the fat and detritus. Decant and transfer to another container to get rid of the residue at the bottom. The broth obtained should be clear and clean.

5. Cook the rice in the broth, either directly in the large pot with all the broth, or in a smaller pot, so as to better control the quantity of liquid. Turn off the heat as soon as the rice is cooked so that it doesn't fall apart (the grains should be well separated but not mushy). Season to taste with salt and mushroom seasoning.

6. Prepare a salad with the chicken meat: traditionally banana blossoms are used, but you can also use cabbage, as shown below.

Serve the soup in individual bowls with chopped scallion and cilantro on the top. Serve the salad on a common plate, with a bowl of *Nước Mắm* Dip* on the side.

REMARKS

If you put the chicken in cold water, the impurities float to the surface better. However, it is said that this method clouds the broth, and that it is preferable to start with boiling water to obtain a nice, clear broth. If possible, choose a good hen rather than a chicken: it will yield a more intense aroma.

To speed things up, you can serve the soup without a salad, shredding the chicken meat and putting it directly in the soup.

The soup needn't be too thick: if necessary dilute it with a bit of water or broth before serving.

Cabbage Salad - Choose a cabbage that isn't bitter (white and compact, like for sauerkraut). Discard the outside leaves, keeping only the tender part. Cut it into the thinnest possible slices. Mix 1 or 2 hours in advance:
- ½ cabbage
- 2 tablespoons white vinegar
- 1 scant teaspoon sugar
- ½ teaspoon salt

Let sit several hours, then press to eliminate the water. Mix with shredded chicken, chopped herbs (*rau răm*), *Nước Mắm* Dip*, and chili pepper to taste. Don't use peanuts.

This salad is not good when prepared at the last minute, as the cabbage is tough and has a strong odor. If you plan to have it for the evening meal, you can start the salad in the morning.

Rice Porridge with Shrimp Balls
Cháo Tôm

There are a multitude of *cháo* variations in Vietnam, the most classic being with chicken (*Cháo Gà**), but you can also make it with clams, meatballs, shrimp... The success of this soup depends on the texture of the rice which shouldn't be too mushy. It's usually eaten as a snack, but it can also be served at the end of a meal.

Serves 6 ~ ⏳ ⏳

- 6 cups Chicken Stock (*Nước Lèo*)*
- ⅔ cup raw rice
- 12 oz raw shrimp
- 1 small shallot
- Pure fish sauce (*nước mắm*)
- Salt, pepper
- 3 scallions (*hành lá*)
- 6 sprigs cilantro (*ngò*)

1. Wash and dry the rice. Toast in a saucepan, stirring constantly with a wooden spatula, until the rice is barely browned.

Cook the rice.

2. Cook the toasted rice in a large volume of water. Turn off the heat as soon as the rice is cooked, so that it doesn't fall apart (the grains should be well detached without bursting; ideally, there will be about ½ inch of broth on the surface). Season with a bit of salt.

Don't cook the rice too much. Like this is fine.

3. In a food processor, combine the shrimp with a small shallot (or a scallion), 1 tablespoon pure fish sauce and ¼ teaspoon pepper, so as to get a very fine paste. Using a teaspoon, form this dough into small irregular balls about the size of an olive. Drop these into the simmering soup and turn off the heat immediately (the shrimp balls cook very fast).

The shrimp dough

Serve in individual soup bowls, garnished with chopped scallions and cilantro. Add a turn of the pepper grinder.

REMARKS

The soup should not be too thick. If necessary, dilute it with broth.

You can use pork (not too lean, shoulder, for example) in place of the shrimp. Season the same way, but let it cook longer.

Variant: if you like a very creamy soup, you can cook the rice for a very long time, or use half regular and half sticky rice.

Islet

Cù Lao

"Islet" is the literal translation of *"cù lao."* This derives from the fact that this soup is traditionally served in a metal pot with a raised center heated by coals. This is a refined dish reserved for special occasions, preferably during the cold season!

Serves 6 ~ ⧗ ⧗ ⧗

- 8 cups very clear Chicken Stock (*Nước Lèo*)*
- 12 raw deveined shrimp
- 1 chicken breast
- 20 small dry shiitake mushrooms (*nấm hương*)
- 1 dry white mushroom (*bạch mộc nhĩ*)
- 2 carrots
- ½ daikon radish
- 1 handful snow peas
- 1 Chinese cabbage (*cải bắc thảo*), white part only
- 3 scallions (*hành lá*)
- 3 sprigs cilantro (*ngò*)

1. Soak the shiitake mushrooms overnight

2. Prepare Chicken Stock* seasoned with salt. At the end of the cooking, add the chicken breast. When the chicken is cooked, remove and shred into strips by hand.

3. Soak the white mushroom for ½ hour.

4. Wash all the ingredients and cut into attractive bite-sized pieces:
   - Carrots into slices
   - Turnip into sticks
   - Snow peas
   - White mushrooms into pieces
   - Shiitake mushrooms (discard the foot)
   - Chinese cabbage into bites 1 x 1 inch
   - Scallions into pieces 1 inch long
   - Shrimp

Dry white mushrooms

The ingredients, ready to cook

Just before serving, cook the ingredients in the broth:

- Start with the shiitake mushrooms, as these take the longest to cook. Wait 5 minutes.

- Then, add the carrots and turnip. Wait 2 minutes.

- Add the rest of the vegetables (snow peas, cabbage, white mushroom). Wait 1 minute.

- Finally, add the shrimp and the scallions.

Serve in a large common bowl, placing the shrimp and chicken on the top. Garnish with cilantro leaves.

REMARKS

If you forgot to soak the dry mushrooms overnight, put them in very hot water for 1 or 2 hours.

You can prepare the stock in advance. On the other hand, the other ingredients must be cooked only right before serving.

The vegetables should be barely cooked so that they are not too soft.

You can replace the chicken breast with pork meatballs.

Bitter Squash Soup
Khổ Qua Hầm

Serves 6 ~ ⧗ ⧗

- 2 bitter squash (*khổ qua*)
- ½ lb ground pork shoulder (not too lean)
- 1 shallot or ¼ onion
- 2 tablespoons pure fish sauce (*nước mắm*)
- ¼ teaspoon pepper

The South Vietnamese are crazy about this very bitter vegetable (those in the North, less so). It is reputed for its medicinal properties: it can be used as a poultice and is also said to purify the blood and cure canker sores.

It is now grown in the West or imported from Thailand. Generally, the tighter the blisters and the darker the color, the more bitter the squash.

1. Prepare the stuffing by mixing the ground meat, chopped shallot (or onion), fish sauce and pepper.

2. Cut the bitter squash in two crosswise. Hollow it with a pointed knife, leaving a cylinder-shaped hole.

3. Stuff the squash with the meat preparation, packing it well all the way into the bottom of the cylinder.

4. In a pot, bring 1 qt of salted water to a boil. Drop in the squash. When the water boils again, lower the heat to medium and skim. Cover and lower the heat some more, letting it simmer gently for about 20 minutes ("*hầm*" means "cooked in a closed environment").

REMARKS

Usually, the resulting broth is very clear. For the stuffing, use more fish sauce than usual, as it will be diluted by the liquid; for this dish, figure 5 tablespoons of fish sauce per lb of meat. You can also use salt in place of fish sauce.

Choose sufficiently large squash, as the small ones are hard to stuff. However, if the squash is too large, the ratio of stuffing to squash will be too high.

Chicken Soup with Bean Threads
Miến Gà

Serves 8 ~

- 14 oz mung bean thread (*miến*)
- 1 hen or chicken
- 1 teaspoon pepper (as an indication)
- 1 tablespoon salt (as an indication)
- 2-inch-long piece of ginger (*gừng*)
- 2 large onions (optional)
- 2 tablespoons mushroom seasoning (optional)
- 3 scallions (*hành lá*)
- 6 sprigs cilantro (*ngò*)

For Vietnamese people, this is a rather ordinary soup which, like *phở,* is often eaten for breakfast, for a snack, or after going to a show.

When served at the table, it is often presented in a large common bowl rather than individual ones: in effect, unlike *cháo gà* which is always eaten as a dish in itself, *miến gà* can be considered a side dish, in the same manner as *canh.*

1. Soak the bean thread a few hours in advance. Though Vietnamese people like to leave it long, as a symbol of longevity, bean thread is easier to handle and to eat when it is cut into pieces 4 to 6 inches long.

2. Place the whole chicken into a pot of salted and peppered boiling water, along with a few peeled ginger slices and the onions, if using them. Cover. Remove the chicken when completely cooked (½ hour to 1 hour). They say that rinsing the chicken briefly under cold water tightens the flesh.

3. When the chicken has cooled a little, shred the flesh and reserve it. Put the carcass back into the pot and boil for about 1 more hour.

4. Remove the carcass from the broth, and skim the surface of the liquid to remove the fat. Decant or filter to eliminate all the residue. The broth should then be clean and clear. Season to taste with salt, pepper and optionally mushroom seasoning.

5. Wash the scallions and cilantro, and chop them coarsely.

6. Bring a large pot of water to a boil. For each guest, drop a handful of bean thread in the pot and cook for about 30 seconds (the bean thread is cooked when it is transparent). Drain and place in a large common bowl or individual ones.

7. Place the shredded chicken on top of the bean thread, sprinkle with the chopped scallion and cilantro, then pour in the broth. Add a few turns of the pepper grinder and serve.

Put a small bowl of pure fish sauce and a some pepper on the table so that each guest can season to taste.

REMARK

The broth should taste strong enough so that the soup isn't bland. In that respect, a hen works better than regular chicken. On the other hand, if the hen flesh is cooked too much, it is not good to eat in a soup. That's the dilemma of chicken soup.

Hanoi Soup

Phở

Serves 6 ~ ⧗ ⧗ ⧗ ⧗

- 2 lb braising beef (short ribs or oxtail)
- 1 lb good, lean beef with no gristle or fat
- 12 oz rice sticks (*bánh phở*)
- 5 large onions
- 1 bunch cilantro (*ngò*)
- 1 star anise (*vị*)
- 1 black cardamom nut (*thảo quả*)
- 1 cinnamon stick
- 2-inch piece of ginger (*gừng*)
- Scallions
- Salt, pepper, pure fish sauce (*nước mắm*)
- Mushroom seasoning (optional)
- White vinegar
- Lemon
- Chili pepper

In the past, this popular dish was never found in a restaurant, small or large. It was sold in small eateries or on street corners. People would eat it on the spot on their way to work, leaning on their bicycle or moped. The top merchants were famous, and always had a line: people would rather wait a while than go to another vendor. The most famous further cultivated their mystique by serving only a fixed number of bowls per day.

This fragrant soup is a specialty of North Vietnam. Beware though: it takes a long time to prepare, and it is expensive! The success of the soup is completely dependent on the broth, which should be subtly fragrant.

The names of the "establishments" were never sophisticated: *Phở Hoà,* *Phở Ngân* (common first names), *Phở Xe Luả* (named after a known place), *Phở Taù Bay* (because the merchant wore an aviator cap!), or *Phở Pasteur* (located on the street of the same name). These eateries have given birth to restaurants with the same names worldwide.

Only since 1975, with the Vietnamese emigration, has *phở* been promoted in rank to a dish worthy of a restaurant. Its success has been such that it is now offered in almost all Asian restaurants, Vietnamese or not.

1. Bring a large pot of water to boil and add the braising beef, salt, and pepper (not too much). Adjust the heat to maintain a vigorous boil so the scum will come up. Skim off the impurities as you go. Add 4 whole peeled onions and the cilantro stalks (set aside the leaves), Lower the heat. Add the star anise, cardamom, cinnamon, and ginger slices in a small cloth bag or strainer so that you can easily remove them later. Keep on skimming, the broth should be really clear.

2. When the broth is nice and clean, cover, leaving a ½-inch gap: if completely covered, the liquid becomes opaque. After ½ hour (more or less, according to taste), remove the spices so the broth won't taste too strong. Let it simmer over low heat for 3 or 4 hours total. Adjust the seasoning with salt.

3. Cook the rice sticks (*bánh phở*) in a large pot of salted boiling water. The cooking time varies depending on the brand (8 to 15 minutes). It's a good idea to check often by pinching a noodle between the thumb and index finger: the noodle should break easily without resisting, but without crushing either. Rinse thoroughly in a colander under cold water. Let drain.

4. Slice the raw beef and the cooked braising beef as finely as possible. It is preferable to prepare the broth the night before, as the cooked meat is much easier to cut after it has cooled. For the raw meat, place it in the freezer to harden it before slicing (around 45 minutes depending on the temperature of the freezer).

The raw meat

The cooked braising meat

5. Thinly slice the last raw onion. Place in a bowl and pour 2 tablespoons of white vinegar on top. Finely mince the scallions and coarsely chop the cilantro.

6. Reheat the noodles in the microwave or by pouring boiling water on them. In the latter case, after draining the noodles, save the broth and bring again to a boil. You can also plunge the noodles in the boiling broth using a small colander.

Place in individual bowls:

- A handful of noodles, filling a bit less than half the bowl.

- Then, on one side, 5 or 6 slices of cooked meat, and on the other side, 5 or 6 slices of raw meat; top with chopped cilantro and scallions.

- Pour the steaming broth on the raw meat and give it a few turns of the pepper grinder.

Place the onion in vinegar, a small bowl of pure fish sauce, and a saucer with lemon quarters and chili slices on the table for everyone to use. This dish should be eaten without delay. If not, the noodles expand, and lukewarm broth is not good.

REMARKS

Avoid using beef shank, as it is very fatty and may soil the broth.

You can, as always, prepare the broth in advance and freeze it. To get a good *phở*, the broth should be fairly concentrated: the meat should fill half the pot of water. If you only use bones, they should more or less be up to the level of the water.

You can plunge the raw meat rapidly in the pot of boiling broth to cook it some, before serving it in the bowls.

Variant - *Phở Gà*: prepare the broth with a chicken instead of braising beef. Then, while assembling the individual bowls, replace the raw beef with shredded chicken meat.

You can cut the onions in two, slice the ginger, and brown them in the oven before dropping them in the broth. This will increase their flavor. On the other hand, the broth might be less clear.

A tip for keeping the meat moist and flavorful: once the braising beef is cooked, leave it to cool in the broth. This also has the advantage of preventing the meat from turning dark. Remove the meat as soon as the broth is cool, so that it doesn't soften too much.

The current trend, gaining ground, though very controversial, is to add all sorts of ingredients to the *phở* such as mung bean sprouts, aromatic herbs (*ngò gai, rau húng quế*), or, the height of heresy, Hoisin sauce! This pleases some and shocks others.

Shrimp Paste Soup

Suông

As with all such dishes, the quality of the broth is essential. The same goes for the shrimp: even though they will be ground, the bigger the shrimp, the more succulent the result.

This soup from the South is considered fancy and distinguished, unlike, for example, *phở*, which is a soup for "everybody." Curiously, it is rarely prepared in the home, being a specialty of street merchants, in the same vein as *phở* or *hủ tiếu*.

Serves 6 ~ ⏳ ⏳ ⏳

- 6 cups Chicken Stock (*Nước Lèo*)*
- 1 handful dried shrimp (*tôm khô*, optional)
- 12 oz rice noodles (*bún*)
- 1 lb medium-sized shrimp
- ½ clove garlic
- 2-inch-long piece of galanga (*riềng*)
- ½ teaspoon salt
- ¼ teaspoon sugar or ½ teaspoon mushroom seasoning
- 6 oz mung bean sprouts (*giá*, optional)
- Aromatic herbs
- 6 sprigs cilantro (*ngò*)
- 3 scallions (*hành lá*)
- Hoisin sauce (*tương ngọt*, optional)

1. Prepare a very good Chicken Stock*. Usually, a handful of dried shrimp is added at the start of cooking.

2. Cook and drain the Rice Noodles (Bún)*.

3. Wash, shell, devein, and dry the shrimp. Add the coarsely chopped garlic and galanga, salt, and sugar. Mix to a fine paste in a food processor.

4. After filtering the broth, bring it to boiling again. With the help of a pastry bag, drop in 2-inch-long cylinders of shrimp paste.

5. Serve immediately in individual bowls:

   - Reheat a handful of noodles by plunging them into the broth, then place at the bottom of the bowl and pour a ladleful of broth on top.

   - Add the aromatic herbs cut into thin slices, and possibly a few blanched bean sprouts.

   - Finally, place a few little cylinders of shrimp paste on top. Garnish with chopped cilantro and scallions, and optionally a little Hoisin sauce or pure fish sauce. Each person adds pepper to their taste.

REMARKS

Do this so that the shrimp paste will be crunchy: before all other preparation, sprinkle salt on the shelled shrimp, let sit ¼ hour then rinse and dry well (don't be lazy, dry them VERY WELL).

Season the shrimp with salt rather than fish sauce, as the liquid would make the shrimp paste less firm.

Pay attention to the quality of the dried shrimp: they should be a pretty pink color and not a dull grey.

Desserts

sponge Cake
Bánh Bò Nướng

Sometimes called honeycomb cake, this was originally a very popular and inexpensive cake sold by street vendors. The current recipe has been adapted by Vietnamese people living abroad.

For 1 cake ~ ⧗

Quantities are specified in grams and milliliters because they must be measured precisely.

- 150 g granulated sugar
- 150 g brown sugar candy (*đường thẻ*)
- 350 ml coconut milk (*nước cốt dừa*) or 300 ml coconut milk plus 50 ml Pandan Leaf Juice (*Nước Lá Dứa*)*
- ½ teaspoon salt
- 150 g tapioca starch (*bột mì tinh*)
- 8 eggs
- 1 tablespoon peanut oil
- 12 g (exactly) baking powder

A successful sponge cake should present a honeycomb pattern with numerous small "chimneys" traversing it from bottom to top. Convection ovens yield the best results.

❧

In a variation *(bánh bò lá dứa nướng)*, the coconut milk is partly replaced by Pandan Leaf Juice*. In that case, brown sugar is also replaced by white sugar.

1. In a saucepan, combine the two sugars, coconut milk, and salt. Bring to a full boil until the preparation becomes thick and syrupy, coating a wooden spoon like liquid honey. This can take a good ½ hour, 45 minutes even. You must watch over it the whole time so it boils without boiling over. Let cool.

2. In another container, mix the remaining ingredients well: tapioca starch, eggs, oil, and baking powder.

3. When the syrup is cool enough that you can dip your finger in without scalding yourself, combine with the preceding mixture, and blend in a food processor until smooth.

4. Pour into a non-stick mold and bake in an oven pre-heated to 355 °F (this is lower than for most cakes) for 45 minutes exactly.

Let cool a little bit before serving (however, it tastes better when served slightly warm).

REMARKS

Never open the oven until the cake is fully cooked; otherwise the dough will sag and won't rise again. You must therefore follow the cooking time exactly. Be sure to center the cake in the oven for optimal rising.

The secret of success is in the sugar syrup, which must be thick enough, otherwise the cake will puff up a lot at the beginning and fall afterwards. Thickening it properly can take a while. The process can be sped up by using only the top, creamy part of the coconut milk. A wide saucepan also helps, but the sides must still be high enough to prevent the syrup from boiling over.

When the egg-tapioca-baking powder mix is added, the syrup must not be boiling (otherwise it will kill the baking powder), but it must be warm enough to promote the rising.

The honeycomb effect is somewhat harder to achieve when using the new soft silicone molds.

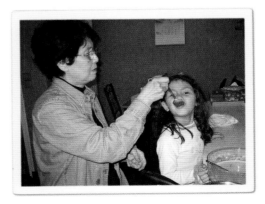

Banana Cake
Bánh Chuối

This very popular cake is sold throughout South Vietnam, especially in markets.

"*Bột tẻ*" is another name for ordinary rice flour (*bột gạo*), whereas "*bột nếp*" designates sticky rice flour. The bananas must be just ripe enough: too ripe, and they will turn black; too green, and the cake will be tart.

For 1 cake ~ ⏳ ⏳

Quantities are specified in grams and milliliters because they must be measured precisely.

Lower layer:

- 4 large ripe bananas
- 200 ml coconut milk (*nước cốt dừa*)
- 200 g granulated sugar
- 1 pinch of salt
- 250 ml water
- 75 g rice flour (*bột gạo* or *bột tẻ*)
- 75 g tapioca starch (*bột mì tinh*)

Upper layer:

- 25 g rice flour
- 25 g tapioca starch
- 125 ml coconut milk

When serving:

- Coconut milk (the creamy part)
- 3 tablespoons sesame seeds (*mè*)
- 1 teaspoon sugar
- ½ teaspoon salt

1. Slice 2 of the bananas into $\frac{1}{16}$-inch-thick disks. Cut the other 2 into three sections each.

2. Separate out the top creamy layer from the coconut milk, and put it aside for later use (when serving the cake).

3. **Bottom layer:** combine the sugar, salt, and non-creamy part of the coconut milk. Add the bananas. Bring just to a boil and then stop. Let cool.

4. Combine the rice flour and the tapioca starch with the water, and then with the cooked bananas. Pay attention, as the flour has a tendency to separate from the water.

5. Pour into a non-stick mold and steam over medium heat for 15 to 20 minutes (or up to 30 minutes if the cake is thick). Wipe the inside of the cover regularly, so that no water drips onto the cake.

6. **Top layer:** Mix the rice flour, the tapioca starch, and the non-creamy part of the coconut milk. Pour onto the cake to obtain a layer about $\frac{1}{10}$-inch-thick. Steam for an additional 5 to 10 minutes.

7. In a pan, toast the sesame seeds until golden colored (but not black), stirring continuously to prevent burning. Add the sugar and the salt. Mash lightly to release the aroma.

Wait for the cake to cool completely before unmolding it. When serving, add a tablespoon of the creamy part of the coconut milk and a pinch of the toasted sesame seeds on each portion.

REMARKS

If the heat is too high, the cake will contain bubbles and blisters.

You can reverse the order of the layers to obtain a different decorative effect.

Layer Cake

Bánh Da Lợn

This spectacular cake, with its contrasting layers, is highly prized by Asians and Westerners alike.

Unfortunately, its preparation is extremely difficult and takes a long time! For this reason, people prefer to make two at a time.

For 2 cakes ~ ⧗ ⧗ ⧗ ⧗

Green layer:

Quantities are specified in grams and liters because they must be measured precisely.

- 0.45 liter Pandan Leaf Juice (*Nước Lá Dứa*)*
- 225 g tapioca starch (*bột mì tinh*)
- 200 ml coconut milk (*nước cốt dừa*)
- 200 g granulated sugar
- ¼ teaspoon salt

Yellow layer:

- 250 g mung beans (*đậu xanh*)
- ⅔ cup water
- 125 g tapioca starch
- 250 ml coconut milk
- 200 g granulated sugar
- ¼ teaspoon salt

1. **Yellow layer -** Soak the mung beans overnight. Cook them over very low heat in a little water, as specified in the list of ingredients. When the water starts boiling, reduce the heat to the lowest level possible and cover. Check that the beans are cooked by pinching one between your fingers: it should crush without resisting. This takes 15 minutes at most.

   Combine all the yellow layer ingredients and blend well to obtain a homogeneous liquid the consistency of a cream sauce. Dilute with some coconut milk if necessary.

2. **Green layer -** Mix all the ingredients for the green layer in a different bowl than the one used for the yellow layer. Add 10 or 15 drops of green food coloring to liven up the color; otherwise the cake will be very dull and unattractive.

3. Bring water to a boil in the bottom of a large steamer. Place a non-stick mold on the top level. Try to maintain a constant temperature:

   - Start by pouring a green layer into the mold. Cover and steam 10 to 15 minutes until the surface is dry. If there is a little remaining water, blot it up with a paper towel.

   - Pour a yellow layer and steam the same way. Generally, the yellow layer won't have the problem of excess water.

Repeat these two steps as many times as necessary until you get the number of layers you want, ending with a green layer. Make the second cake in the same way. Some steamers have three levels, allowing you to cook two cakes at the same time.

Let cool before unmolding (however, this cake is eaten slightly warm). Cut in slices or dice just before serving.

Flexible molds can be used to get varied shapes.

REMARKS

This cake freezes well. Before serving, it's necessary to let it thaw completely for 24 hours, then reheat it in a microwave, making sure that the green part has become transparent again. At this point, the cake is a bit too hot to eat and should be left to cool slightly before serving.

It is important to use two ladles of equal volume for the two colors. Each layer should be about ⅛-inch thick. Typically, cakes sold in stores have five layers, but good cooks will make a point of producing a cake the same thickness with nine layers.

Mung Bean Cake
Bánh Đậu Xanh Nướng

This traditional cake is a bit heavier than the others and is best enjoyed with tea, perhaps, rather than after a meal.

This cake is truly foolproof—perfect for beginners!

For 1 cake ~ ⧖
- **7 oz mung beans** (*đậu xanh*)
- **⅔ cup water**, approximately
- **7 oz granulated sugar**
- **⅚ cup coconut milk** (*nước cốt dừa*)
- **3½ oz tapioca starch** (*bột mì tinh*)
- **½ teaspoon salt**

1. Soak the beans overnight (the amount of water used isn't important).

2. Drain the beans and cook over low heat with little water (the water level should cover the beans by about ½ inch). Once the water boils, reduce heat as much as possible and cover. The beans cook fast, in 15 minutes at most. Test by pinching one bean between your thumb and a finger; it should crush without resisting.

The cooked beans.

3. Let cool. Add the sugar, salt, coconut milk (preferably the creamy upper part of the container), and flour.

4. Process in a blender until you get a very fine and homogeneous batter. Pour into a non-stick mold.

5. Bake at 425 °F in a preheated oven. After 10 minutes, poke about 20 little holes in the cake to ventilate the crust; otherwise the cake will inflate and won't look good.

Bake 45 to 50 minutes. Check periodically by poking with a knife: as with other cakes, when the knife comes out clean, the cake is done.

REMARKS

This cake tastes better when it is lightly browned. Wait several hours before serving, otherwise it will difficult to cut.

The cake will keep several days to a week in the fridge or can be frozen. It will be necessary to microwave it just before serving, so that it regains a soft consistency.

Cassava Cake

Bánh Khoai Mì

For 1 cake ~ ⧗

- 14 oz frozen grated cassava (*khoai mì bào*)
- 7 oz granulated sugar
- 1 ¼ cup coconut milk (*nước cốt dừa*)
- ¼ teaspoon salt

This traditional cake, extremely simple to prepare, uses grated cassava *(khoai mì bào),* and not the usual cassava flour *(bột mì tinh).* Previously, you had to grate the tuber yourself, but luckily, frozen grated cassava is now available.

1. Combine all the ingredients and mix well. If for some reason the mix is too liquid, add a little (1 tablespoon) tapioca starch (*bột mì tinh*).

Frozen grated cassava

2. Pour the mix into a non-stick mold about 8 inches in diameter.

3. Cook in a 390 °F preheated oven for 40 minutes. Monitor the progress by sticking a knife into the middle of the cake. When the knife comes out clean, the cake is ready.

REMARK

This cake is good when it is lightly browned. It can be frozen without problems. It should be reheated in a microwave just before serving in order to regain a soft consistency.

Sugar Cookies

Bánh Phục Linh

These little cookies, very popular in South Vietnam, are unknown in the North (as are all dishes with coconut, for that matter).

Children love them, but some people find them difficult to swallow. In fact, there is a technique for that: instead of putting a whole cookie in your mouth, bite off a small piece and let it melt on your tongue!

They can be eaten anytime, but they complement tea or coffee particularly well. Handle with care: they are fragile!

For 30 cookies ~ ⏳ ⏳
- 3 ½ oz pandan leaves (*lá dứa*)
- 7 oz tapioca starch (*bột mì tinh*)
- ⅓ cup coconut milk (*nước cốt dừa*)
- 3 ½ oz powdered sugar

1. Cut the pandan leaves into 1-inch-wide strips, perpendicularly to the fibers.

2. In a non-stick skillet, cook the leaves and tapioca starch over very low heat until the leaves become brittle. Stir constantly, so the starch stays white and does not stick. Sift once or twice through a very fine sieve to remove any leaf crumbs.

3. Let cool COMPLETELY (this is mandatory; if you don't, there will be lumps, and the cookies will be ruined). Add the powdered sugar, then pour in the coconut milk drop by drop while kneading continuously. Keep on kneading for a long time. We want a very fine, damp dough that is not mushy or lumpy.

4. Fill each mold with the dough and pack firmly with your thumbs. Turn the mold over and tap the end lightly to free the cookies.

The cookies keep up to a week in the refrigerator (watch out: coconut milk has a tendency to turn sour with the heat). They can also be frozen: you will need to put a paper towel between each layer of cookies to prevent sticking. They can be thawed by leaving them for a few minutes at room temperature. They can also be eaten frozen.

A collection of wooden molds

There are also plastic molds!

REMARKS

The cookies can be left white or colored with food coloring. Traditionally very pale pastel colors are chosen: pink, light blue, pale green... Before putting in the molds, divide the dough into separate bowls and add a drop of food coloring to each. This adds to the work, as you must again knead the dough for a long time to keep it uniform. You can also

add the food coloring to the coconut milk, which is somewhat easier.

Sometimes the cookies are put in the oven. These cookies are less fragile, but alas, also less tasty.

Agar-Agar Jello Cake
Bánh Sương Sa

Although agar-agar is eaten frequently in Vietnam, many are not familiar with this uncommon cake, which used to be sold by only a few street vendors. It is nonetheless easy to prepare and keeps well. Some makers created works of art by inlaying little items or entire landscapes of contrasting colors in the center of a transparent cake.

With the help of fancy silicon molds, you can easily produce spectacular, finely "sculpted" cakes.

> **For 2 cakes ~** ⧖
> - 2 oz agar-agar (*sương sa*)
> - Granulated sugar to taste
> - Coconut milk (*nước cốt dừa*)
> - Food coloring
> - Fancy molds

1. Soak the agar-agar 3 or 4 hours in cold water, then cut into 1-inch-long pieces. Drain.

2. Divide the pieces into several parts that will be cooked separately in order to obtain assorted colors and tastes.

   - **Transparent layers:** in a saucepan, place 1 part agar-agar to 2 parts water. Add sugar to taste and, possibly, some food coloring (traditionally pink or green).

   - **Opaque layers:** substitute coconut milk for the water. Don't add sugar.

   In both cases, bring to a boil, then lower the heat, cooking over low heat until the agar-agar is fully dissolved. Stir from time to time.

3. Assemble the cakes following your inspiration. The agar-agar will set when cooled. You need to wait until one layer is dry to the touch before pouring the next. In the meantime, keep the pots of agar-agar covered to avoid hardening.

The simplest way to assemble this cake is in layers with alternating colors. Pop any bubbles with a toothpick.

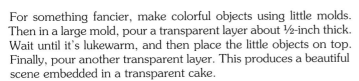

For something fancier, make colorful objects using little molds. Then in a large mold, pour a transparent layer about ½-inch thick. Wait until it's lukewarm, and then place the little objects on top. Finally, pour another transparent layer. This produces a beautiful scene embedded in a transparent cake.

REMARKS

Cutting the agar-agar into little bits is mainly a way to measure its volume.

This cake will keep several days in the refrigerator.

Floating Dumplings
Bánh Trôi Nước

For 15 dumplings ~ ⧗ ⧗

- ⅔ cup water
- 1 cup dried mung beans (*đậu xanh*)
- 1 tablespoon vanilla-flavored sugar (optional)
- 1 lb glutinous rice flour (*bột nếp*)
- 2 tablespoons sesame seeds (*mè*)

Syrup:

- 4 cups water
- 1 lb brown sugar bars (*đường thẻ*)
- 1 large piece ginger (*gừng*)
- 1 pinch salt

This spectacular dessert is, in the end, not as difficult to make as it looks.

Figure one ball per person. Some people are able to eat two, but they are rare!

1. Soak the mung beans overnight.

   Drain and place in a saucepan, add the water. Bring to a boil, and then set on lowest heat. Optionally, add the vanilla sugar. After 5 or 10 minutes, turn off the heat. Crush the beans with a spoon: you will rapidly get a paste resembling a thick purée.

   Form the bean paste into balls about 1 inch in diameter (this must be done while the beans are still warm, since it becomes difficult when they are cold). Let cool.

Soaked beans

Bean purée

2. In another bowl, put the glutinous rice flour and carefully pour in warm water (104 °F), kneading until you get the consistency of soft modeling clay. Form this dough into balls the same size as the previous ones.

3. Prepare a syrup by bringing to a boil the water, the brown sugar, and the ginger (peeled and thinly sliced). Add the salt and turn off the heat.

   Roast the sesame seeds in a pan over medium heat, making sure they don't burn. (Watch out, it goes fast!)

4. Bring to a boil a large pot ⅔ full with water.

   Take a rice ball in the palm of your hand and place a bean ball on top. Squeezing gently, progressively wrap the sticky rice around the yellow bean ball. Roll between the palms of your hands to spread the outer dough evenly. The resulting dumpling will be roughly the size of a ping-pong ball.

   Place the dumplings in boiling water and allow to cook over medium heat for about 10 minutes. When a ball floats to the surface, leave it in an additional 30 seconds, then gently fish it out with a wire net and drop it in the sugar syrup.

5. Just before serving, take the dumplings out of the syrup, sprinkle them with sesame seeds, and place in individual bowls. Gently pour some syrup into each bowl, taking care not to fully cover the dumplings (otherwise the sesames seeds will float off).

REMARKS

If there is leftover rice flour dough, make little marble-sized balls with a small piece of brown sugar in the center. Cook them with the others, and serve a big dumpling with a small one. Watch the happy surprise when the guests bite into it and taste the liquid syrupy center!

You can present the dumplings in a large common bowl, but then the sesame seeds might fall off.

Corn Pudding
Chè Bắp

This dessert is very easy to prepare. However, don't use canned corn, as this treat is tastier when the kernels are scraped and a bit broken.

❧

Choose tender white corn, neither too ripe nor too young. To select an ear, peel back the husk and press a few kernels, verifying that they are neither too hard or soft. If they creak a little, the corn is good!

Serves 8 ~ ⧖

- 4 fresh ears of corn
- 1 cup sticky rice (*gạo nếp*)
- Sugar to taste (5 oz typically)
- ½ teaspoon salt
- ⅔ cup Pandan Leaf Juice (*Nước Lá Dứa*)*
- ¾ cup coconut milk (*nước cốt dừa*)

Pandan leaves, present in numerous desserts, give a nice aroma and a characteristic tint.

1. First, slice the corn off the cobs, holding the knife at an angle with the ear, not cutting too deep. Then, scrape firmly, holding the knife perpendicularly to the ear, to get the rest: the kernels must be broken, not whole. Throw away the cob, of course!

2. Carefully wash the rice and cook it in 4 times its volume of water, uncovered. When the water boils, add the corn. Let it boil gently for around 10 minutes, making sure the rice is cooked just right (the corn cooks faster anyway).

3. With the heat still on, add the sugar to taste, salt (1 or 2 pinches) and the Pandan Leaf Juice*. Adjust the consistency by adding water if necessary.

4. Turn off the heat as soon as the mix boils. This *chè* should have the consistency of a thick porridge (like *cháo*), the top staying a bit liquid.

When serving, add a tablespoon of coconut milk on top of everyone's bowl.

REMARKS

If in doubt, it's best to use less water when cooking, as it is easier to adjust the consistency by adding water than by removing some!

Don't overcook the rice, otherwise it disintegrates. We don't want mush.

Some like to replace the rice with tapioca pearls. It cooks faster, but tastes different.

Sweet Soup with Tapioca Sticks
Chè Bột Khoai

Bột khoai is a dried tapioca starch formed into straight sticks or zigzags. It is only one of the numerous ingredients in this typical South Vietnamese dessert, which, unlike most such dishes, requires a lot of work.

It is usually eaten in the evening, often preceded by a bowl of *cháo gà* for a light dinner. The street vendors carry a pot of *chè* on one end of a shoulder rod, and small bowls on the other end, together with a little lamp. They set up in front of a theater, or wander in the streets, calling, *"chè bột khoai!"*. They sit on the ground to serve their customers.

Serves 6 ~ 🍵 🍵 🍵

- ⅔ cup mung beans (*đậu xanh*)
- ⅓ cup tapioca pearls (*bột báng*)
- 40 dried lotus seeds (*hạt sen*)
- ⅔ cup dried seaweed (*phổ tai*), cut into small pieces or 1 large piece 8 in x 1 in
- ⅔ cup Chinese dates (*táo tầu*), dried and pitted
- 4 pandan leaves (*lá dứa*)
- ⅔ cup dried shredded tapioca (*bột khoai*)
- Granulated sugar (5 oz approximately)
- ⅓ teaspoon salt
- 1¼ cup coconut milk (*nước cốt dừa*)

1. Soak separately overnight: the mung beans, tapioca pearls, lotus seeds, and seaweed. Don't use too large a piece of seaweed, as its size will triple!

The dates

2. The next day, soak the dates (1 hour is enough), then drain all the ingredients that were soaked overnight. Rinse the seaweed thoroughly, then cut it into pieces $^1/_{16}$ x 1 inch.

The seaweed

3. In a pot, cook the beans in double their volume of water. As soon as the water boils, lower the heat to a minimum. Stop the cooking before the beans burst (at most 15 minutes).

The cooked beans

4. Cook the tapioca pearls in three times their volume of water. Turn off the heat as soon as they are transparent (3 to 5 minutes maximum).

5. Place the lotus seeds in three times their volume of water. Cover and cook over low heat for about 45 minutes, so that the seeds are tender in the mouth, but still whole. Save the cooking water!

6. In a large pot, boil the pandan leaves tied in a knot for 10 minutes in 2 qt of water. Add the sugar. When the liquid boils again, add the tapioca sticks. Test the cooking progress by pinching, as for pasta. This will take a few minutes at most.

7. When the tapioca sticks are cooked and transparent, add the rest of the ingredients, including the cooking water from the lotus seeds. Add the tapioca pearls at the end to prevent them from sticking together, and the coconut milk at the very last.

8. After the last ingredient has been added, bring to a boil and then turn off the heat. Adjust the soup's consistency by adding water as needed: it should be a lot more liquid than the other *chè*. Taste and add sugar if necessary.

9. To serve: pour a small ladle of liquid into each bowl, then add a ladle of the rest, making sure there is a little bit of everything. Don't eat the pandan leaves!

REMARKS

Bring the liquid to a final boil after all the ingredients have been added. Otherwise, the *chè* might sour.

Watch out, the tapioca has a tendency to stick to the bottom of the pot. It's important to stir constantly with a wooden spatula.

Banana Pudding
Chè Chuối

Serves 12

~ ⧗

- ⅔ cup tapioca pearls (*bột báng*)
- 6 large ripe bananas
- Sugar (5 oz approximately)
- Salt
- Coconut milk (*nước cốt dừa*), about 1 cup
- 2 tablespoons sesame seeds (*mè*)

Chè is a kind of pudding with the consistency of a thick soup. This one can be prepared in 10 minutes from start to finish. You simply need to pay attention and not let the tapioca pearls cook too much. Also, choose bananas that are ripe just so: too ripe and they turn black, not ripe enough and they are tart, the dessert will be bland.

1. Soak the tapioca pearls overnight. The next day, drain and discard the water. Bring to a boil a volume of water equal to five times that of the pearls (before soaking), then throw in the tapioca pearls. Stir continuously: if you don't, the tapioca will stick to the bottom. Turn off the heat as soon as the pearls have become transparent (3 minutes).

2. Cut the bananas in pieces about 1½ inches long. Cook them in a little water (so they are immersed but not drowned) for 3 minutes.

3. Combine the cooked tapioca and the bananas (along with the cooking water from the bananas). Add sugar to taste and ½ teaspoon of salt. Turn off the heat.

4. Open the container of coconut milk without shaking it. Gently scoop up and set aside the creamy part on top. Pour ½ cup (or more, according to taste) of the clear juice from the bottom into the dessert. The mix should be somewhat liquid, as it is going to thicken.

Some people advocate cutting the bananas into small slices...

5. In a small pan, roast the sesame seeds until they turn golden (but not black), stirring continuously so that they don't burn. Add a scant teaspoon of sugar and ½ teaspoon of salt. Mash lightly to release the aroma.

Serve in individual bowls: one piece of banana and a few spoonfuls of tapioca (according to each person's taste). At the last moment only, top each bowl with a small tablespoon of the coconut cream and a pinch of roasted sesame seeds.

REMARKS

There is no need to use a large amount of tapioca, as it swells enormously when cooked!

The cooking water must be boiling when you add the tapioca, otherwise the pearls may become mushy. The tapioca bought in Asian markets won't cook well unless soaked overnight. "Western" tapioca doesn't have that requirement.

Don't hesitate to turn off the heat even if the tapioca pearls aren't yet completely transparent, and a white dot remains in the middle: they will continue to cook a bit. If overcooked, they might become sticky and lumpy.

Since the tapioca keeps expanding and thickening after cooking, it is best that the result be a bit liquid. On the other hand, it is preferable not to start with too much water, as it is easier to add some than to remove some!

Black Eyed Pea Pudding
Chè Đậu Trắng

Serves 8 ~ ⏳ ⏳

- ⅔ cup black eyed peas (*đậu trắng*)
- 1 tablespoon baking soda (optional)
- ⅓ cup glutinous rice (*gạo nếp*)
- Sugar to taste (5 oz approximately)
- 1¼ cup coconut milk (*nước cốt dừa*)
- 1 pinch salt

This is a treat from the South, as are practically all the coconut-based desserts. In general, they can be gotten from street vendors.

The black eyed pea is actually a legume: it becomes mellower when soaked in baking soda.

1. Soak the black eyed peas overnight, possibly with added baking soda.

   Soak the rice separately. The exact amount of water is not important.

2. Rinse the peas in cold water, then cook them in a large volume of water. When the water is red, drain the beans into a sieve and rinse. Put them back in the pot with fresh water and cook some more, repeating the operation two or three times until the water stays clear.

   When the beans are cooked (about 20 minutes total cooking time), remove from the heat and drain.

3. Rinse the glutinous rice in cold water. Cook it in 3 times its volume of water. Stop the heat as soon as the rice is cooked (the grains become translucent without bursting). A bit of water is likely to remain, but don't bother to drain it.

4. Mix the black eyed peas and the rice; add sugar to taste, salt, and coconut milk. If necessary, add some water in order to get the consistency of a slightly watery *cháo*: you need to have at least 1 inch of liquid on the surface, since the preparation will expand a lot.

Taste and add sugar if necessary. Serve warm. You can add a teaspoon of the cream from the coconut milk on top of each bowl.

REMARK

It is important to remove the rice from the heat as soon as it is cooked.

Tapioca Pudding

Chè Đậu Xanh Bột Bán

This pudding, typical of South Vietnam, is but one amongst the numerous *chè*. Rather than a dessert, *chè* is considered a treat: and in fact, the expression *"chè cháo"* is used to designate such foods you indulge in.

❧

Although this is not traditional, you can add a cup of *Pandan Leaf Juice (Nước Lá Dứa)** when mixing the two other ingredients.

❧

The quantities are for reference only, as the qualities and consistencies of the ingredients will vary from brand to brand. You need to watch, taste, and adjust.

Serves 6 ~ ⧖ ⧖

- ⅔ cup mung beans (*đậu xanh*)
- ⅓ cup tapioca pearls (*bột bán*)
- 1 pinch of salt
- ¾ cup coconut milk (*nước cốt dừa*)
- Sugar to taste (5 oz typically)

1. Soak the beans and the tapioca pearls separately overnight.

2. Cook the beans in an equal volume of water (volume of beans measured after soaking and swelling of the beans) over very low heat; as soon as the water boils, lower the heat to a minimum, cover, and wait about 10 minutes. Crush with a spoon or in a food processor to obtain a very fine paste (this is not necessary if the mung beans are very fine).

3. In another pot, bring to a boil a volume of water 3 times that of the tapioca pearls (before soaking), then pour in the pearls and lower the heat so that it is boiling very weakly. Stir continuously. As soon as the pearls are a bit translucent, they are done. Don't hesitate to turn off the heat, even if the centers are still a little white: the tapioca will continue to cook for a while.

4. Mix the bean paste and tapioca in a non-stick pot and return to the heat. Add the salt and coconut milk. Mix well. Add the sugar slowly, to taste. Bring to a boil, stirring continuously: if you don't, it will stick badly. Turn off the heat.

Now, here is the secret to success: When turning off the heat, you should see at the bottom of the pot a somewhat solid layer, the consistency of thick pudding; above that, 1 inch of liquid. The liquid will eventually be absorbed by the bottom layer, which is going to expand. The proportions are critical: if there is not enough liquid, the pudding will be compact; if there is too much liquid, it's not good either.

REMARK

If in doubt, it's best to use less water. You can always add some later.

Taro Pudding

Chè Khoai Môn

Taro roots are found in all sizes, from small to very large. In this recipe, we'll use little brown ones, the size of an average potato.

Serves 6 ~ ⧗ ⧗

- 5 small (potato-sized) taro roots (*khoai môn*)
- ⅔ cup glutinous rice (*gạo nếp*)
- 1 pinch salt
- Sugar (5 oz approximately)
- ⅔ cup Pandan Leaf Juice (*Nước Lá Dứa*)*
- ¾ cup coconut milk (*nước cốt dừa*)

1. Cook the taro roots unpeeled in boiling water for about 20 minutes. Check the progression by sticking a fork in the roots: cooked taro has the same consistency as a boiled potato. Peel the taro roots and cut into 1-inch-wide cubes.

2. Cook the rice, using about 2 parts water to 1 part rice. Once done, the rice should have the consistency of a thick *cháo*: if necessary, add some water during the cooking. Turn off the heat as soon as the rice is cooked; the grains should not burst.

3. Add 1 or 2 pinches of salt, sugar to taste, and the taro cubes.

4. Add the Pandan Leaf Juice* and the coconut milk. The mix should now have the consistency of a very liquid *cháo,* because it is going to thicken.

REMARKS

In a recent interpretation, *gạo nếp* is replaced by *cốm dẹp*. This is tastier because *cốm dẹp* is fragrant, but, of course, it costs more...

Instead of mixing in the coconut milk with the rest, you can bring it to the table in a large bowl or several individual small ones. Then everyone can add it to their taste.

If in doubt, it's best to use less water for the cooking, as more can always be added later.

Banana Fritters
Chuối Chiên

A must for children! Like all the other banana desserts, fully ripe bananas are required, or they will be bland.

❧

The addition of baking powder and a little potato starch in the batter yields a light and crunchy fritter.

Serves 6 ~ ⧗ ⧗

- 6 ripe bananas
- 10 heaping tablespoons wheat flour
- 1 tablespoon potato starch (optional)
- 2 teaspoons baking powder
- Water
- Peanut oil

1. Combine the flour, the baking powder, and optionally the potato starch. Stir in water little by little, until you get a fairly liquid batter that flows smoothly without breaking. Whip the batter for a long time to make it very smooth. Let sit for 30 minutes.

2. Heat the oil in a saucepan. Coat each banana by dipping it into the batter and then fry it, making sure there is enough oil to completely immerse the banana.

3. Remove the fritters and drain them on a paper towel.

Sprinkle with sugar and serve immediately.

REMARK

Once cooked, the fritter should be light and crunchy: if the fritter is hard, the batter was too thick. If the batter spreads in the oil, it was too liquid.

Sticky Rice Wine

Cơm Rượu

Cơm Rượu (or *rượu nếp*) is a treat made from fermented sticky rice. It has a very sweet taste and the distinctive fragrance of rice alcohol. Very popular in Vietnam, it is eaten as a dessert or between meals as a snack. The street vendors serve bowls of *xôi vò*, on which they place a few balls of *cơm rượu* and a spoonful of juice. In the North, cooked rice is left to ferment in a jar as is, whereas in the South, it is formed into little balls first.

The special yeast for rice wine is found in all Asian grocery stores that sell Vietnamese products.

Serves 12 ~ ⧗ ⧗

- 1 lb raw sticky rice (*gạo nếp*)
- 9 balls of yeast for rice wine (*men cơm rượu*)
- ½ teaspoon salt

1. Soak the raw sticky rice for 3 or 4 hours in cold water, then drain.

2. Spread the rice on the upper level of a steamer and steam for around ½ hour. The result should have the consistency of regular steamed rice, a bit wetter than *xôi*.

3. Spread the cooked rice on a platter in a ½-inch-thick layer and let it cool.

4. Crush the yeast balls into powder. Sprinkle it evenly on top of the rice while it is still warm.

5. Dissolve the salt in a cup of water. Wet your hands with the salty water. Taking small amounts of rice, form balls 1 inch in diameter. Pack them firmly so they don't fall apart during fermentation. Place the balls in a glass container.

6. Seal the container hermetically; for example with several layers of plastic wrap. This is imperative for a good fermentation. You can first cover the rice balls with a banana leaf, or even stick pieces of banana leaf between the balls.

7. Place the container is a warm place (near a radiator, a heating vent, or in an oven set to 85 °F, no more).

After three days, the balls will be ready, bathing in a transparent sugary and fragrant alcoholic liquid. Serve 3 balls and a spoonful of the liquid. Traditionally this is accompanied by a plate of *xôi vò*.

This preparation keeps for a few days in the refrigerator, no more.

Although you can cook the rice in a pot, it is preferable to use a steamer. This allows better control of the amount of water that is absorbed, and turning off the heat as soon as the rice has reached the desired consistency.

Stuffed Sticky Rice

Xôi Nhưn Đậu Xanh

For 4 rolls ~ ⧗ ⧗

- ⅔ cup mung beans (*đậu xanh*)
- 1 cup raw sticky rice (*gạo nếp*)
- 2 tablespoons peanut oil
- Grated coconut
- Granulated brown sugar
- Creamy part of coconut milk (*nước cốt dừa*), optional

Imagine... At breakfast time, a street vendor sits in front of your house. In a precut piece of banana leaf, she spreads successively a layer of sticky rice, a little bean paste, grated coconut, and finally a small spoonful of brown sugar. She then closes the whole construction by folding the leaf, and hands it to you.

Instead of a banana leaf, you can use *bánh tráng phồng*. This rice paper sheet, similar to *bánh tráng*, is made with sticky rice that expands when roasted. Once softened, it can be used to roll food. This Vietnamese product has recently become available in Asian markets.

The frozen grated coconut used here is now very conveniently available in Asian grocery stores.

1. Soak the mung beans and rice overnight in separate containers.

2. Mix 1 or 2 tablespoons of oil with the rice so it doesn't dry out. Cook it (covered) in a steamer with small regularly spaced holes. This operation is fairly quick: 10 to 15 minutes. Crush a grain between your fingers to check that the rice is tender. You can, during the cooking, sprinkle 3 tablespoons of water over the rice.

3. Cook the beans over low heat in very little water (just enough to immerse them). Watch out, mung beans boil over easily! Then, crush the beans with a spoon to make a coarse paste.

4. On a sheet of plastic wrap, spread a rectangular layer of rice. Place a little bean paste on top, then some coconut, and finally the sugar.

5. Roll it up to close it and form a roll the size of a spring roll. Eat warm or cold.

REMARKS

If the holes in the steamer are too big, you can place a piece of cheesecloth on the bottom to prevent the rice from falling through.

A nice touch: when serving, add a spoonful of coconut cream on top of the roll (use the thicker top part in a can of coconut milk).

Basic Preparations

Rice Noodles

Bún

Together with a platter of aromatic herbs, these noodles are the ideal companion to many grilled meat or fish dishes. As they are soft, they can also replace angel hair pasta (*bánh hỏi*), which is more difficult to store. Numerous soups (*bún bò Huế, suông, bún mắm,* etc.) use *bún* as a base.

- 1 package rice noodles (*bún*)
- 1 cup Scallion Oil (*Mỡ Hành Lá*)*

1. Bring to a boil a large pot of water with salt added. It is best to break the noodles in half because, even though they may not look very long, after cooking, they become elastic and difficult to handle. Cook them for 5 to 10 minutes, testing continuously as they have a tendency to turn to glue. Watch out, cooking times can vary considerably between different brands!

2. Strain and rinse immediately under running cold water for 30 seconds at least. Let them drain for a long time.

3. Cover with Scallion Oil* before serving.

The rinsing will, of course, cause the noodles to be cold. You can reheat them in the microwave oven just before serving. However, in Vietnam, cold noodles are generally preferred, especially in days of intensely hot days.

REMARKS

There are different types of *bún*. The closest to Vietnamese *bún* is "*bún Quế Lâm,*" straight and fine.

As for any pasta, use a lot of water for cooking.

These noodles are best when well drained: wait at least a half-hour before serving to allow water to evaporate.

A nice touch (that also makes it easier to eat): place the noodles on the serving platter in swirls like little bird's nests.

212

Steamed Rice

Cơm Trắng

Whenever possible, choose Thai "fragrant" rice. In Vietnam, there are some significantly better species (*gạo tám thơm, gạo nanh chồn, gạo nàng hương, etc.*). Their grains are two or three times smaller, and the rice is exceptionally light and fragrant. Unfortunately, these are not available abroad.

- Raw rice
  (⅔ cup for two servings)
- Water

Rinse the rice several times, then drain. Cook it (without adding salt to the water):

- **In a pot:** use a volume of water 1½ times that of the raw rice. Bring to a boil, then immediately lower the heat. Don't cover yet (it may overflow). Once the rice has absorbed all the water, lower the heat to a minimum, then cover. Wait about 10 minutes.

- **In the microwave oven, using a special microwave rice cooker:** volume of water is 1½ to 2 times the volume of rice. Microwave time is 11 minutes for 2 servings (⅔ cup of raw rice), 18 minutes for 4 servings, 21 minutes for 6 servings.

- **In an electric rice cooker:** follow the manufacturer's instructions (usually 1 volume of water per volume of rice).

Microwave rice cooker.

REMARKS

"Steamed rice" is actually not steamed!

Never serve packed rice: air it all the way to the bottom of the pot using a fork or chopsticks.

Burnt crispy rice is a real treat. Once the water is completely absorbed, let it cook on lower heat an additional 20 minutes. Serve the upper part per usual, and when you get to the bottom, add some Scallion Oil* and a bit of salt; detach the circular rice cake and divide the crispy pieces between the diners.

The required volume of water varies with the type of rice: for "new harvest" rice, only one volume of water per volume of rice is needed.

Pickled White Turnip
Củ Cải Dầm Nước Mắm

This dish is served mainly with *bánh tét* (Southern version of *bánh chưng*), and is a practically required accompaniment. It is also eaten in the morning with plain rice porridge (*cháo trắng*).

For this preparation, never use black turnips, which are compact and not very crunchy. White turnips can be found in all Asian markets: Chinese, Vietnamese, Japanese...

- Pure fish sauce (*nước mắm*), approximately 1 cup
- 1 tablespoon sugar
- 1 cup water
- 1 large white turnip, 8 to 12 inches long

1. Peel the turnip, cut it in sections 1½ inch long, then split each section into 8 pieces lengthwise.

2. Place the pieces on a heat source until they are completely dry and shriveled. This can take 24 to 48 hours.

3. Fill a jar a bit more than halfway with the pieces.

4. Boil the water and sugar. Turn off the heat. Add the fish sauce, stir, and taste. The liquid should be fairly salty because the turnip by itself is bland. Let it cool.

5. Pour the liquid into the jar containing the turnip pieces. The turnip will expand a lot, but not regain its initial volume.

Let sit at least a week before consuming.

REMARKS

In Vietnam, the water, fish sauce, and sugar are boiled at the same time. This is smelly and accomplishes nothing, since cooked fish sauce is not as good.

As a precaution, store this preparation in a cool place. Unopened, it will keep for several months.

You need to dry the pieces of turnip rapidly to avoid mildew.

Aromatic Herb Platter
Dĩa Rau Sống

Many Vietnamese dishes must be accompanied by a large platter of salad and aromatic herbs. This is, in fact, a distinctive touch in Vietnamese cuisine that brings freshness and originality.

tía tô

rau giấp cá

- Large salad leaves (batavia or lettuce)
- Polygonum (*rau răm*)
- Mint (*rau húng*)
- Perilla (*tía tô*)
- Vietnamese basil (*rau húng quế*)
- Fish herb (*rau giấp cá*)
- Cilantro (*ngò*, optional)

---

1. Wash and drain all the ingredients.
2. Remove the larger stems, leaving groups of 2 or 3 leaves.
3. Cut the salad into pieces around 2 x 4 inches.

Place everything on a wicker or lacquer tray, grouping the herbs by type. The herbs must be abundant and form a small mountain!

REMARKS

You can prepare the platter a few hours in advance: in this case, cover with a damp kitchen towel to prevent drying. However, it's preferable to prepare it at the last moment, because after 1 or 2 hours, the herbs wilt a bit.

Rau giấp cá is indispensable to the South Vietnamese. In the North, only connoisseurs eat it…

Cilantro is not normally included in the platter, being principally used as a garnish. However, some people appreciate its characteristic fragrance and like to present it together with the other herbs.

rau húng

rau răm

ngò

rau húng quế

Pickled Bean Sprouts
Dưa Giá

This preparation is extremely common in Vietnam among all the social classes. It is eaten mainly with dishes like *Thịt Kho** or *Cá Kho**, whose salty flavor mixes well with the tartness of the brine. Less wealthy people used to soak these in *nước mắm* and eat them with rice. These are mung bean sprouts (*giá đậu xanh*) and not soybean sprouts, as they are often called by mistake.

- 1 lb mung bean sprouts (*giá đậu xanh*)
- 2 scallions, white part only (*hành lá*) or ½ onion, minced
- 1 qt water that was used to wash rice

1. Wash the scallions. Only keep about 2½ inches of the lower white parts of the stalks. Place them at the bottom of a glass or porcelain container. The scallion helps with the fermentation.

2. Wash the sprouts well and get rid of any non-fresh brown pieces. Drain and place in the container with the scallions.

3. Pour in the water from the rice washing, enough to immerse the sprouts.

4. Cover and let macerate at room temperature for 1 or 2 hours.

   Skim the white film that forms on the surface, and then drain the sprouts. This preparation will keep 3 or 4 days.

REMARKS

The sprouts should be fresh and very white, not brown, otherwise they'll rot. At the market, lift them in your hand and spread your fingers to "sift" them, letting any dubious pieces drop.

Traditionally, the sprouts are macerated only in rice water. The film that forms on the surface is expected. You can eliminate it completely by rinsing the sprouts after maceration, but then, they won't taste as good.

In place of the rice water, you can use 1½ tablespoons salt diluted in 1 qt fresh water. The result is tidier, but there again, the taste is less pronounced.

216

Mắm Nêm Dip

Mắm Nêm Pha

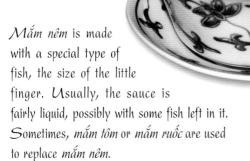

Mắm nêm is made with a special type of fish, the size of the little finger. Usually, the sauce is fairly liquid, possibly with some fish left in it. Sometimes, *mắm tôm* or *mắm ruốc* are used to replace *mắm nêm*.

The best *mắm nêm* is produced in Central or South Vietnam. Its quality shows in its fragrance, which must be pronounced, but not so strong as to be unpleasant.

- ½ cup *mắm nêm*
- 1 stalk fresh lemongrass (*sả*)
- 1 lemon
- 1 tablespoon sugar
- ½ cup water

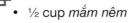

Chop the lemongrass finely and juice the lemon. Mix well all the ingredients, adding water progressively: you will obtain a fairly thick sauce because of the lemongrass. Taste and adjust the seasoning if necessary.

REMARK

The sauce must be salty, yet mild. It should get to your throat!

Mắm Ruốc Díp - Mắm Tôm Díp

Mắm Ruốc, Mắm Tôm Pha

Accompanied by a bowl of Steamed Rice* and a few slices of cucumber, this preparation, also called *"mắm phệt,"* serves as an emergency meal. As a condiment, it is very suitable for different sorts of fondues.

In the South, a distinction is made between *mắm tôm,* which is brown and made from little shrimp, and *mắm ruốc,* which is purple and made from another very tiny crustacean.

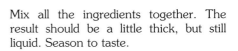

For 1 cup

- 2 scant teaspoons *mắm ruốc*
- 2 teaspoons sugar
- 2 teaspoons vinegar
- 10 teaspoons water

Mix all the ingredients together. The result should be a little thick, but still liquid. Season to taste.

REMARK

A brand that is frequently used is *mắm ruốc chà Huế.*

Scallion Oil

Mỡ Hành Lá

This preparation is completely indispensable. It gives flavor to angel hair pasta (*bánh hỏi*) and other noodles in general.

It also prevents food from drying out, especially when reheating.

For 1 cup

- 12 scallions (*hành lá*, also known as "green onion")
- 1 cup peanut oil

Slice the scallions into small rounds ($1/10$-inch thick).

Heat the oil in a saucepan, making sure you don't let it smoke. Test by throwing in a piece of scallion: if it sizzles, the temperature is right.

Throw the white rounds into the oil first and the rest a few seconds later. Turn off the heat immediately.

REMARK

This preparation keeps a long time in the refrigerator. You can also freeze it without any problem.

Pandan Leaf Juice

Nước Lá Dứa

This preparation, present in numerous desserts, confers a very characteristic aroma and color. Pandan juice can sometimes be found as a frozen concentrate, but it is always very disappointing, as is the commercially produced pandan essence. Nothing replaces freshly homemade juice from the leaves!

For 1 qt of juice

- 3½ oz pandan leaves (*lá dứa*)
- 1 qt water

1. Cut the leaves into small pieces, then put them in a blender with half the water. Process for a long time. Filter.

2. Add the rest of the water, and blend again until there are practically only white fibers left. Filter again.

REMARK

This preparation keeps several months in the freezer.

Chicken Stock - Pork Stock

Nước Lèo - Nước Dùng

The robust pork stock can be used for fondues, but for soups, the more refined chicken stock is preferred. Ginger is always present in Vietnamese chicken stock, albeit in very small quantities. You can, according to taste, add a handful of dried shrimp or finish the seasoning with a spoonful of mushroom seasoning.

Chicken Stock:

- 1 raw chicken
  or 2 raw chicken carcasses
  (ask the butcher to quarter
  them)
- 3 large onions
- 2-inch-long piece of ginger,
  peeled and sliced
- 1 scant teaspoon salt
- 1 scant teaspoon pepper

Pork Stock:

- 4 lb pork bones
- Salt and pepper
- 3 onions

REMARKS

Stock is used as a base in many recipes. Since it takes a long time to cook, it is good to prepare it in advance and freeze it for later use.

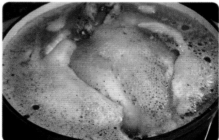

It is imperative to skim the stock clean.

1. Bring a large pot of water to a rolling boil. Add all the ingredients. Boil over high heat and skim the surface of the stock for 10 minutes.

2. Cover, lower heat, and simmer for 3 hours. Important: Don't cover completely; place the cover to leave a gap a fraction of an inch wide. If the pot is completely covered, the stock will become opaque.

3. Decant or filter before using.

Nước Mắm Dip

Nước Mắm Pha

This is the ubiquitous accompaniment for all dishes. It can be used for seasoning dishes, or presented on the table, in small individual bowls; each person dips the bites of food in it before eating. In Vietnam, lemon being rare, lime is used almost exclusively. Some people replace it with vinegar.

For 1 cup

- 4 tablespoons pure fish sauce (*nước mắm*)
- ½ lemon, pressed
- 1 heaping tablespoon sugar
- 1 garlic clove, peeled and crushed
- Chili pepper, chopped or sliced (optional)
- ½ cup water

Mix all the ingredients. Be sure to taste and adjust the seasoning, since pure *nước mắm* can be more or less salty, and everyone's taste is different.

REMARKS

If possible, use *nước mắm "Phú Quốc 35°"* and beware of imitations! Pay attention as well to the concentration: you will find 25° and 35°, 35° being a lot better.

If you substitute vinegar for the lemon, the sauce will keep longer. However, it is tastier with lemon.

Peanut Sauce

Tương Pha

Although the traditional ingredient for this preparation is soybeans, you get good results with less effort using Chinese Hoisin sauce.

Peanut sauce is absolutely indispensable for *Gỏi Cuốn**, *Nem Nướng**, *bánh khoái,* as well as many other dishes.

- 6 oz Hoisin sauce
  or 1 can salted yellow soybeans
- 1 heaping tablespoon raw sticky rice (*gạo nếp*)
- 2 tablespoons toasted peanuts
- 1 scant teaspoon mushroom seasoning (optional)
- Sugar

---

1. Rinse the sticky rice. Cook with ⅔ cup water as for normal rice (over low heat, or it will stick).

2. Crush the peanuts very finely.

3. Mix all the ingredients in a blender. Adjust the consistency by adding water in order to obtain a uniform creamy texture that is neither too thick nor too liquid. (It should coat the spoon.)

4. Adjust the seasoning with a bit of sugar if necessary. Don't add salt, as the soybeans are salty enough.

Serve in small individual bowls, sprinkling more crushed peanuts on top at the last moment. Offer some chili peppers on the side.

Ingredients
and Utensils

Utensils

Vietnamese cuisine doesn't really require any special utensils: what you need foremost are good knives, cutting boards, and patience! You will notice while reading along that non-traditional appliances (microwave oven, blender) are mentioned when their utilization doesn't degrade the result.

On the other hand, here is a list of tools that, while not essential, make life quite a lot easier for the cook.

Electric Rice Cooker

Sold in all appliance stores, this device produces perfectly steamed rice without the need to watch over it, and as a bonus, keeps it warm.

Microwave Rice Cooker

This little plastic pot, which appeared recently, is specially designed to steam rice in the microwave oven in about 15 minutes. For small quantities, it can replace the classic electric rice cooker.

Steamer

This utensil is indispensable for steaming. The upper steamer basket is set on top of a pot of boiling water. If you are buying one, choose it big enough to hold a cake, with holes small enough that sticky rice can be cooked without the grains falling through.

Standard Rice Bowl

The ubiquitous so-called "watermelon seed bowl" is handy for measuring volumes, since there is always one lying around. Its volume is roughly 250 ml or 1 cup.

Fondue Nets

These accessories allows everybody to cook and fish out their ingredients easily from a fondue pot. They are indispensable for guests who have trouble handling chopsticks.

Flat Ladle

This ladle was designed for frying flat fritters such as *Bánh Tôm**.

Electric Grill

Much more practical than a barbecue, it can serve as an outdoor as well as indoor grill.

Raw Rice Measuring Container

Rice cookers come with a "standard" measuring container of 16 cl or ⅔ cup.

*Bánh Phục Linh** Mold

Made of wood or plastic, it is sold in Asian supermarkets.

Silicon Molds

They are quite convenient when it comes to unmolding cakes after they are cooked. The little ones can be used to make the small items to be included in *Bánh Sương Sa**.

Peanut Grinder

This little gadget grinds peanuts to the ideal size for use in numerous dishes.

Pâtés Chauds* Mold

This fairly common little device can help close the Pâtés Chauds tightly.

Vegetable Grater

This ingenious grater will cut carrots and papayas into strands for salads. Of all those we have tested so far, this one produces the best results!

Fondue Stove

This little stove placed in the middle of the table keeps the fondue broth boiling. As it uses a small gas canister for fuel, there is no cumbersome electric wire.

Tô

Not to be confused with the earthenware *tô*, the *tô* is a bowl a bit larger and more flared than a regular rice bowl. It is used for soups.

How to Set the Table

Anyone who has attempted to eat with chopsticks may have found themselves like the stork in the Aesop fable, incapable of grasping anything in its long beak. When eating with chopsticks, you need a bowl! It is acceptable, even necessary, to seize the bowl in the left hand while the right hand uses the chopsticks to push the food, rice in particular, into the mouth.

Therefore, the place setting on the table for each guest should include a rice bowl on a small plate, chopsticks to the right, and in front a small bowl for the dipping sauce. For soup, use a *tô*.

While some dishes are served in individual portions, more often the food is placed in the center of the table in a large common platter. In this case, you take a small amount of food, eat, then help yourself again, and so on. Never grab a full serving right from the beginning.

Bạc hà – Taro stalk

Also known as "elephant ear stalk" and called "*dọc mùng*" in North Vietnam, this vegetable consists of a large leaf at the end of a long stem. Only the stalk is eaten, cut into diagonal slices. In soups, its porous texture allows it to soak up broth like a sponge!

Bạch mộc nhĩ – White mushroom

It is only found in dried form. After soaking and cooking, it is slightly crunchy but rather bland. It is said to have medicinal virtues.

Baking soda

Used to soften some ingredients and as an aid to digestion; it is available in any grocery store.

Bánh canh – Translucent noodle

These are the Vietnamese equivalent of udon noodles. The dough needed for making these typical Southern noodles is prepared by washing a large ball of kneaded flour under running water. This has the effect of eliminating some of the starch, making the dough transparent, and giving the noodles their special consistency - somewhat firm to the bite. The noodles, as fat as a chopstick, are very long and slightly tapered at the ends, no doubt due to the artisanal fabrication method. You can buy them fresh in Asian markets, vacuum packed. These are definitely better than the frozen or dried ones.

Bánh hỏi – Rice vermicelli

Also called "angel hair," these rice noodles belong to the same family as the more common *bún*, but they are much thinner. They are tastier when fresh, but difficult to find. Otherwise, buy them frozen. To preserve their texture, reheat rapidly in a steamer and cover with a bit of scallion oil before serving.

Bánh phở – Rice stick

Known also as "rice noodles," these typically Vietnamese flat noodles can be wide or narrow. The word "*phở*" comes from the North. In the South, "*hủ tiếu*" designates both the noodles themselves and the dishes prepared with them. *Bún* and *bánh hỏi* are also members of this family: *bún* is finer than *phở* with a round cross section, and *bánh hỏi* is finer still.

Bánh phồng tôm – Shrimp cracker

Also called "shrimp chips," they are prepared with a base of ground shrimp. These crackers expand dramatically when plunged into hot oil. They are normally intended as a snack with drinks, but people got in the habit of serving them with *gỏi* in place of the traditional grilled *bánh tráng*.

The frying oil should be just the right temperature. If too hot, the chips burn and harden without expanding correctly; if too cool, they don't expand well either. They should be taken out of the oil as soon as they puff up.

Once fried, they can be stored in a sealed plastic bag. Beware: some brands are clearly better than others! There is a similar product made with crab (*bánh phồng cua*).

Bánh tráng – Rice paper

These are the wrappers used for making the various rolls, in particular, the celebrated imperial roll (*chả giò*) and the equally famous spring roll (*gỏi cuốn*). As the rice paper is already cooked, you need only soak it to soften it, and then roll the food and eat.

The traditional way of making these is very much like pancakes: rice batter disks are poured onto a cloth stretched over a pot of boiling water, steamed, and then left to dry in the sun. In the countryside you will still find woven bamboo racks used for this purpose. This method of drying produces a very characteristic crosshatch pattern on the paper.

Depending on the brand, the rice paper is more or less sturdy. The stronger ones are easier to handle, but can be tough when eating (this is the case for those containing tapioca flour). Ideally the rice paper should be strong enough so it doesn't break, but still feel soft in the mouth.

There is a special variety of *bánh tráng* that is grilled and used to accompany salads. These are thicker and often include sesame seeds or grilled onions.

Bắp chuối – Banana blossom

In South Vietnam, the word "*bắp*" means a long object with tapered extremities like a muscle. In particular, "*bắp ngô*" means an ear of corn, "*bắp chuối*" a banana blossom (in the North, we say "*hoa chuối*").

The banana blossom is located at the extremity of the banana bunch. Inside, between the petals, are small undeveloped bananas that are usually discarded, since they often taste bitter. Banana blossoms are used as a vegetable, particularly in chicken salad.

Banana blossoms are sold in all Asian supermarkets, fresh or canned. To preserve the fresh flower's pretty pink color, plunge it into water with vinegar as soon as you take it out of its airtight container. The canned flowers are, frankly, just as good and a lot easier to use.

Bắp ngô – Corn

In South Vietnam, they say simply "*bắp*" and in the North, "*ngô*," but the correct term for corn is "*bắp ngô*." It is a very popular treat. Little vendors carry boiled ears of corn, still hot, in a wicker basket and offer them on the street or in the market. In the evening you'll find them on the sidewalk, grilling the corn on a small brazier, basting the ears with scallion oil one by one on demand, and salting them just before handing them to the customer.

As a general rule, white corn is preferred because it is more tender. To choose an ear, pull back the husk and press on the grains to check that they are neither too hard nor too soft. If they crack a little bit, they are good. Canned corn may be substituted for fresh corn, but grated fresh corn is much tastier as for everything else.

Bard

The type of bard used in our recipes can be bought from the butcher. It is the same stuff that is wrapped around roasts or pâtés. In Vietnam, before using, it is spread out in the sun until it becomes translucent. It is useful to give a nice texture to meat or shrimp balls.

Bì – Pork rind

See "*Da bì*."

Bò – Beef

In Vietnam, cattle are raised only in the plateau regions, since the weather is too hot in the South, and there are no suitable grazing areas. As beef is expensive, it is consumed much less frequently than pork and often cut into very small pieces. In the countryside especially, they never ate beef in the old days.

- Braising beef: this is used for stock. If possible, select short ribs. You can also use shoulder or neck, but avoid the shanks, as they are very fatty and may foul the broth.

- Tender beef: for the fondues and *phở*, a good cut of meat such as eye of round is required. You can also, of course, use fillet, which is better still.

Bột bán – Tapioca pearls

This product is always made with tapioca flour, which is manioc (also called cassava) starch. The tapioca beads swell a lot and continue to thicken even after cooking. Hence it is not necessary to use a large quantity.

The tapioca bought in Asian markets does not cook well unless soaked overnight. Western tapioca has less need of soaking. In both cases, water must be brought to a boil before throwing in the pearls. If they are thrown in cold water, they may become mushy. You can also find crushed *bột bán* that is usable immediately (it is not in the form of little balls, but after cooking, the final consistency is the same).

Bột bánh bao – Steamed bun flour mix

Bánh bao is not deemed a success unless after cooking, the dough is white, smooth, and light. The choice of flour is therefore particularly important. It is safest to use a flour specially formulated for *bánh bao*.

Bột bánh xèo – *Bánh xèo* flour mix

Although you could prepare the *bánh xèo* batter yourself, you can save time by buying a ready-to-use mix from Asian markets.

Bột chiên tôm – Fritter flour mix

This mix can be used for all the fritters: *chuối chiên*, *tôm chiên*, *bánh tôm*, etc. You can also easily formulate it yourself with wheat flour, some baking powder, and a little bit of potato starch.

Bột gạo – Rice flour

This flour is prepared similarly to wheat flour, by grinding raw rice. It is the most widely used flour in Vietnam and constitutes the base of numerous cakes. You can also find it under the name "*bột tẻ*." Be sure not to confuse it with other types of rice flour such as *bột nếp*.

Bột khoai – Dried shredded tapioca

Bột khoai is cassava starch (see "*Bột mì tinh*") dried and sold in the form of sticks the size of kitchen matches, sometimes colored and cut in fanciful ways.

Bột khoai mì – Tapioca starch

See "*Bột mì tinh*."

Bột khoai tây – Potato starch

Although it appears in some recipes, potato starch is not native to Vietnam: the potato is rare and not cultivated there except on the high plateau, where it is a bit colder. This starch helps to make fritters or meatballs crunchier.

Bột măng thích – Crumbly rice flour

Instead of being in powder form, this flour contains little dry lumps, like small pebbles. Before using, knead it with water.

Bột mì – Wheat flour

Not to be confused with "*bột khoai mì*"! Wheat is not native to Vietnam and no traditional Vietnamese cakes use it. Wheat flour mainly appears in dishes adapted from foreign recipes, particularly French ones. Outside Vietnam, it is used more frequently, as it is more readily available than the traditional Vietnamese flours.

Bột mì tinh – Tapioca starch

To be precise, tapioca is the flour obtained from the tuberous root of the cassava plant, which is also called manioc.

In the past, "*bột mì tinh*" and "*bột năng*" designated distinct flours, made from two different tubers (*củ*): *củ năng* and *củ mì tinh*. Today, these two flours translate to "tapioca starch" and are probably both made from cassava root (*khoai mì*).

The plants that produce the three tubers in question (*củ năng, củ mì tinh, khoai mì*) don't resemble one another at all, but the flours have similar properties, allowing to use them interchangeably.

Bột năng – Tapioca starch

See "*Bột mì tinh*."

Bột nếp – Glutinous rice flour

This flour is prepared with sticky rice or *gạo nếp*, also known as "glutinous rice." It exists under several variants.

Bột tẻ – Rice flour

"Bột tẻ" designates exactly the same ingredient as "bột gạo," that is, plain, ordinary rice flour. On the other hand, bột nếp is flour made from glutinous rice.

The correct terminology uses the words "gạo tẻ" for regular rice and "gạo nếp" for sticky rice, but nowadays these are abbreviated as "gạo" and "nếp."

Bún – Rice noodle

Presented with a platter of aromatic herbs, these noodles constitute the ideal accompaniment to a large number of dishes, particularly grilled meats. Tender, they can replace bánh hỏi, which is harder to find and doesn't keep well. Many soups (bún bò Huế, suông, bún mắm, etc.) have a base of bún as well.

Various types and brands of bún are available in Asian food stores: the one closest to Vietnamese bún is sold under the brand name "Quế Lâm" (Vietnamese translation of "Guilin," a well-known region in China). Once cooked, it most closely resembles fresh Vietnamese bún. It works particularly well for chả cá or bún chả. In soups, the quality of the bún is less important.

Bún tàu – Mung bean thread

See "Miến."

Bưởi – Grapefruit

Whenever possible, buy pomelo, a large Asian grapefruit that is abundant in Vietnam. It peels easily, and its thick pulp does not collapse. It is less bitter than a normal grapefruit, and sometimes downright sweet!

Cá bông lau – Catfish

Catfish is one of the most commonly eaten fish in Vietnam. It appears in numerous recipes from the simplest to the most sophisticated. There are many different varieties of catfish:

- cá bông lau: a large fish with black skin, raised both in Vietnam and in the United States. There are several variants of it: in the United States, it is sold under the name "catfish"; if imported from Vietnam, it is slightly different and sold under the name "basa." This type of fish was introduced in Vietnam relatively recently, but it seems to have supplanted the older species (cá trê et cá tra).

- cá trê: smaller than cá bông lau, has firmer flesh and costs more. It is often marinated in nước mắm and ginger, and then cooked whole over a wood fire.

- cá tra: although it resembles cá bông lau considerably, it is considered a poor man's fish, with less firm flesh and a grey skin that sometimes has an unpleasant odor. Nevertheless, it is commonplace among Vietnamese people to think that cá bông lau and cá tra are the same fish.

Cá lóc – Snakehead fish

Cá lóc is rather close to pollack or hake in its shape and taste, only much better! Its round body is about 15 inches long and covered with scales the size of small fingernails. Its head is flat, which led to the name "snakehead fish."

This is a very good fish with fine flesh, firm and succulent. In Vietnam, it is reputed to be the most digestible of all fish and often reserved for children and the sick. Carefully save the tail and head for making soup; unlike other fish, it doesn't have a strong smell.

Cá lóc, like cá bông lau, is sold whole frozen. You may also find it in slices, which is more convenient.

Cá thác lác – Notopterus

This little flat fish, the size of a hand, has astonishing properties! Its light taste makes it suitable for delicate soups. When its flesh is pressed and scraped with the back of a spoon, it quickly acquires an elastic yet crunchy consistency. It is little known in North Vietnam. You can find it frozen in Asian supermarkets.

Cá tra – Catfish

See "Cá bông lau."

Cá trê – Catfish

See "Cá bông lau."

Cà chua – Tomato

Formerly, tomatoes were not widespread in Vietnam: they were used mostly in the cities, in expensive dishes. As is the case for many western vegetables, the best tomatoes grew in Dalat, in the central highlands of the South. In other places, they were grown in kitchen gardens, but most of the time, the fruits were small and not very good-looking. They are in greater use these days.

Cà cuống – Essence of mangdana

Greatly appreciated by the people of North Vietnam, this essence is extracted from the glands of a large insect. This product costs literally its weight in gold, so it is used extremely sparingly: dip the point of a toothpick into the tiny glass vial of cà cuống, then put it in the bowl. This is sufficient to flavor a whole bowl of food or dipping sauce! You can now find artificial cà cuống, the best of which, we have to admit, comes fairly close to the real thing.

Cà ri – Curry spices

The Vietnamese have fully adopted curry, adapting it in their own way. They are not, however, as demanding about it as the Indians, who were responsible for introducing it to Vietnam. In the South, coconut is added, but not in the North.

Cà rốt – Carrot

Abroad, it is often used in gỏi. In Vietnam, it was once a rare and expensive vegetable, grown only in the highlands around Dalat. Although it is more widespread now, you should avoid using it at every turn: a few strands can add a pleasant touch of color that nicely complements the green of other ingredients in gỏi, but carrots shouldn't be the main ingredient.

Cà tím – Eggplant

Eggplant is a popular vegetable widely used in Vietnam. When possible, use the flavorful Asian eggplant, easily recognizable by its elongated shape and lighter color.

Cải băc thảo – Napa cabbage

Also called Chinese cabbage, this is an oblong and compact cabbage, one of the numerous green vegetables used in Vietnamese cooking. Enjoy it in salad, cooked, or pickled.

Cải bẹ trắng – Bok choy

This vegetable exists in numerous forms, the most common being a dark green spoon-shaped leaf at the end of a light-colored stalk.

The word "*cải*" means "leafy vegetable." There are many varieties of *cải* and they are used in many different ways: sautéed, boiled, in soup, or in salads.

Cải bẹ xanh – Chinese mustard

A very popular vegetable from the mustard family (the word "*bẹ*" designates vegetables with a large stalk, such as chard). If it is young, it is eaten raw with *thịt kho* or *bánh xèo*. Otherwise, it is sautéed or used in soup. Its strong taste marries well with fish, in particular *cá rô* (tilapia) and in the South, *cá thác lác*.

Another extremely common way to prepare *cải bẹ xanh* in North Vietnam is to dry it whole on strings. Once dry, but not too dry, it is put in brine and takes on a saffron color. Prepared this way, the vegetable has a sour taste with a crunchy stalk. You can wash it a little to reduce its bitterness, and then cut it into small pieces. It is eaten sautéed with beef or in soup with a little pork. With cold rice, it is a good after-school snack. You can also use it to accompany *thịt kho* or *cá kho*, since salty and sour combine well.

Cải cúc – Chrysanthemum leaf

See "*Rau tần ô.*"

Cải làn – Chinese broccoli

This vegetable differs from regular broccoli by the presence of flowers and edible leaves as well as a stronger flavor. Its round stalk is tender and succulent.

Chả lụa – Vietnamese pork roll

This cooked sausage, about four inches in diameter, originated in North Vietnam (where it is called "*giò lụa*"). It is made with loin meat from freshly slaughtered pigs: it was traditionally men's work to pound the meat by hand until it looked like dough. Nowadays, the South Vietnamese and the Thais also produce it, with varying degrees of success.

Chanh – Lemon

The yellow lemon is practically nonexistent in Vietnam (except in certain cooler regions like Dalat and the high plateau) and lime prevails. Nonetheless, if lemons are more readily available, we'll use them because, in the end, it makes little difference whether it's lemon or lime.

Chim cút – Quail

In Vietnam, quail is a luxury food reserved for high-ranking dinner guests. It is often served with an expensive special rice, *gạo tám thơm*.

Chuối – Banana

In the Vietnamese landscape, banana trees stretch as far as the eye can see and the varieties are numerous. There are also wild banana trees that typically produce small fruits, and you will notice a cluster of banana trees behind every house. There is a proverb that goes, "Plant areca nut in front of the house and banana in the back."

Bananas are usually eaten raw. A single variety is cooked: the small chubby "pig banana," which is eaten as a treat. Banana blossoms are also consumed (*bắp chuối*).

Cốm dẹp – Green glutinous rice

If this rice is harvested as it should be, that is, before maturity, the inside of the grain has a pretty light green tint. If it is harvested late, no matter how much colorant is added by the producer, the consistency and aroma will never be the same: the real *cốm dẹp* is very tender with an aroma of pandan leaf. Unfortunately, this aroma dissipates with time and will be gone by the time the product reaches the store.

After harvesting, the fresh rice is roasted rapidly in a large skillet, then husked and more or less flattened (*dẹp*). As it is already cooked when purchased, it can be eaten as is: you need only moisten it a bit and wait for it to soften and reveal its fragrance, then it's ready to eat as a treat. It can also be used to make numerous fragrant cakes. It is expensive because the yield is low.

Unfortunately, this type of rice is only available during the harvest season, when tender rice is harvested. You will find in all Asian supermarkets a product sold under the name "*cốm dẹp*," but usually that is crushed and colored rice and not at all the authentic product. Though it is usable for lack of a better alternative, the true *cốm dẹp* cannot be found outside Vietnam. It's even hard to find it there!

Cơm cháy – Crispy rice

This was originally the burnt residue at the bottom of the rice cooking pot. It is so popular that the Vietnamese sometimes will burn the rice on purpose.

If you have a pan that doesn't stick too much, do this: once the water is absorbed, lower the heat so the rice doesn't burn entirely, while leaving it high enough so that the rice fries lightly and becomes crusty. For this, you need to wait a while longer (20 minutes) than regular cooking. Serve the rice as usual, and when you get to the bottom, add some scallion oil and a little salt, then detach the fried rice cake and serve it.

You can sometimes buy crispy rice already seasoned, ready to eat. However, this is difficult to find.

Củ cải – Daikon radish

Turnips and radishes are very common in Vietnam. They are found in many shapes, sizes and colors. In general, they are eaten cooked or pickled, but you can also find them in salads. The leaves are equally good to eat, particularly in soups.

The daikon radish is a long white radish with very thin skin that resembles a giant white carrot. The black radish is similar, but is uncommon in Vietnam, as is the round turnip.

Củ sắn – Jicama

Jicama is a vine native to Central America. Only the tuber is eaten, as the rest of the plant is very toxic. Its creamy white juicy flesh, rather crunchy, is a bit similar to that of the pear. Normally it's eaten raw in salads, but it can also be cooked, in particular for the stuffing of chả giò. When it is not available, carrot can be substituted.

Cua – Crab

Crab, ubiquitous in Vietnam, is particularly abundant in the South: near Nha Trang or Huế, you have ghẹ with fine succulent meat; in the far South, the ghẹ gives way to a blue variety resembling the Dungeness crab.

In Europe, tourteau or spider crab is used, as its meat is most like that of Vietnamese crab. The American Dungeness crab is equally good, but nothing compares to ghẹ! You sometimes find it frozen in Asian markets. It has the advantage of being easy to peel thanks to its tender shell.

Figure a good half hour to shell one crab. It you are pressed for time, buy king crab if you can find it: it's excellent, though costly. As a last resort, Asian markets will sell frozen Canadian "snow crab" in little 1-lb blocks.

Da bì – Pork rind

The word "bì" means "skin" in Sino Vietnamese, so, in fact, the expression "da bì" is redundant. In Vietnam, fresh pork rind is used, which must be cleaned at length. Fortunately, three types of ready-to-use pork rind are now available: fresh (the best), frozen (suitable), and dried (last choice as it's yellow, smelly and takes a long time to wash).

Dấm – Vinegar

Alcohol vinegar isn't used in Vietnam, nor is red vinegar in general. On the other hand, you can find rice vinegar, which is sweeter than wine vinegar, and even banana vinegar!

Dầu hào – Oyster sauce

This is a Chinese sauce based on oysters, salt, flour and sugar. It is commonly used by the Vietnamese. There also exist vegetarian equivalents.

Dầu – Oil

In Vietnam, lard and peanut oil are the most common types of shortening. The latter is good at high temperatures and thus ideal for frying and sautéing. Olive oil, whose flavor is completely foreign to Vietnamese cuisine, is to be absolutely avoided.

Dừa – Coconut

See "Nước cốt dừa."

Đậu bắp – Okra

A popular vegetable widely used in the Vietnamese countryside, where it grows readily. It is usually eaten dipped in the sauce of a salty meat dish. To get rid of the slimy texture, add a bit of lemon or vinegar.

Đậu nành – Soy

Here we mean the real soy, the one used in particular for soy milk and tofu. What is usually called "soy" or "soybean sprouts" is in fact đậu xanh or mung bean.

Đậu phộng – Peanut

In Vietnam, peanuts are eaten in all forms! Boiled, they are sold by street vendors who walk about at all hours with a large basket that can be more or less hot, handing them out in paper cones. Roasted and salted, they serve as munchies with drinks. Raw, they are a vegetable, mixed with other vegetables, for example in the stuffing for a duck.

If necessary, you can use the roasted-salted appetizer peanuts, but ideally, unsalted peanuts are preferred.

Đậu phụ – Tofu

See "Tầu hủ."

Đậu trắng – Black eyed pea

This dry bean is exactly the same as the black eyed pea. In Vietnam it's found only in chè. To make the beans creamier, soak them in baking soda.

Đậu xanh – Mung bean

Đậu xanh is erroneously called "soy" or sometimes "green bean," although its proper name is "mung bean." Hulled and split, it resembles yellow lentils. When whole, it is a bright green round seed. Generally, "đậu xanh" refers to the hulled bean, as the whole bean is seldom used.

Đu đủ – Papaya

This fruit grows everywhere in Vietnam and is sold by the hundreds of thousands in the markets. It is eaten green or ripe, raw or cooked. Poor families add bits of green papaya during the cooking of meat to tenderize it.

Green papaya is used mainly and extensively in salads, for example with shrimp or grilled dried beef.

Đường – Sugar

In Vietnam, only cane sugar is used. There are three types: refined white, brown in the form of small bars (*đường thẻ*), and finally, brown granulated sugar (*đường cát mỡ gà*), which is creamier. In the South, you will see a lot of sugarcane plantations with their own refineries.

For several decades, the deplorable trend in the South has been to add sugar everywhere. Likewise, the abuse of MSG has become unbearable!

Đường thẻ – Brown sugar bar

Also sold as "sugar candy," these are in the form of brown bars, sometimes with two colors, approximately 6 x 1.25 x 0.25 in. They are much more flavorful than white sugar.

Gạo – Raw rice

In Vietnamese, having a meal (*ăn cơm*) means literally "eating rice." This underscores the fact that rice is the basic staple of the Vietnamese diet, and as a consequence, numerous words describe it in all its forms. In particular, be sure not to confuse: *gạo* (raw rice) and *cơm* (cooked rice).

In times past, the poor ate essentially rice and vegetables. In lieu of milk, babies would get the water that had been used to cook the rice. Even in the richer families, meals always included many bowls of rice, and on average three dishes: a vegetable soup, a meat dish, and a dish of boiled vegetables, or more often, sautéed with onions. Even in well-to-do families today, the mothers feed rice to their children very early on: the rice is cooked for a long time in a lot of water to soften it, then a bit of pork fillet and some soy sauce are added.

The so-called "perfumed" Thai rice is the preferred type. In Vietnam, some species are significantly better, but they can never be found abroad (*gạo tám thơm, gạo nanh chồn, gạo nàng hương*, etc.). Their grains are two or three times smaller than those of ordinary rice; once cooked, they are remarkably light and fragrant.

Gạo nếp – Glutinous or sticky rice

Glutinous rice is a special variety of rice, also called, not very correctly, "sticky rice." *Cốm dẹp* is obtained by harvesting *gạo nếp* before maturity while the grains are still green.

Giá – Soybean or mung bean sprout

The term "*giá*" usually designates mung bean sprouts. In theory, there is a distinction between true soybean sprouts (*giá đậu nành*) and mung bean sprouts (*giá đậu xanh*). Vietnamese people rarely eat soybean sprouts, but mung bean sprouts are quite common. This is especially true in the South, where the unfortunate tendency is to toss them into every dish, even those where sprouts are not used traditionally, such as *chả giò* or *bánh xèo*.

Gừng – Ginger

Ginger is cheap in Vietnam. Technically speaking, it is a rhizome, that is, the underground stem of a plant. Every Vietnamese family has ginger in the garden! As it grows close to the surface, a piece is easily picked off when the need arises. It can also be kept frozen. It is an indispensable ingredient in chicken broth. Young ginger (*gừng non*) is consumed raw or marinated in vinegar.

Hành hương – Shallot

The plain shallot is widely cultivated in Vietnam. It is often fried and used as a garnish for vegetables or main dishes, like *bánh cuốn*.

Hành lá – Scallion

Known also as green onion. Don't confuse them with chives: scallions are longer and fatter, with stalks .2 to .4 inches in diameter, the lower end being white. They are ubiquitous: before serving, main dishes or soups are always garnished with a little handful of chopped scallion and cilantro.

Hành phi – Grilled shallots

Dried grilled shallots are sold in bags or in plastic boxes in Asian markets.

Hạt sen – Lotus seed

You find them dried, in packets or on strings. The best seeds, fragrant and tender, come from Huế, but you can find lotus seeds everywhere from the North to the South.

Hẹ – Chinese chive

This variety of green onion is used rather like a vegetable, in soups for example, or sautéed together with bean sprouts. Its presence is indispensable in several dishes such as *gỏi cuốn* and *nem nướng*. The stalks are flat and more rigid than those of ordinary green onion, with a pronounced garlic taste. They are used in both raw and cooked dishes.

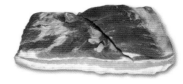

Heo – Pork

Pork is the most frequently consumed meat in Vietnam. The usual dishes containing meat (*thịt kho*, soups, *cháo*, sautéed vegetables with meat) are therefore prepared with pork. For those who can afford it, There is meat at every meal.

Thịt ba rọi - pork belly:
It is almost always boiled. Frequently used in *gỏi*, always with *mắm,* it is essential for *mắm kho*! *Thịt kho*, on the other hand is normally prepared with fresh leg of pork. Pork belly should be boiled long enough to become tender. To save time, one might be tempted to cut it in pieces or cook it without the rind. However, since the rind contributes to the flavor, it's better to cook a large whole piece of meat and dole it out later in small slices.

Hột điều – Cashew nut

The fruit of the cashew tree is yellow and the size of an apple. Its skin is thin, bright, and smooth with red highlights. This very pretty fruit is edible, but it is much less prized than the nut that is attached underneath it.

Khô bò – Dried beef

This Vietnamese equivalent of beef jerky is sold in plastic packets in all Asian markets. The meat is in the form of thin slices, rather spicy, with various seasonings: five spices, lemongrass, or fruits. Pork prepared in the same manner is now available.

Khô cá thiều – Dried fish

Cá thiều is a species of fish that is more commonly found dried than fresh. You'll see mountains of it in the markets of the big towns in the Mekong delta. It is eaten mainly as a snack.

Khổ qua – Bitter squash

Also called *mướp đắng*, this squash is renowned for its medicinal properties: it serves as a poultice for feverish children and is also said to purify the blood and heal canker sores.

The South Vietnamese are crazy about this bitter vegetable; those in the North... less so. It can be found abroad, grown locally, or imported from Thailand. In general, the tighter the blisters, the more bitter the squash. The seeds aren't eaten.

Khoai lang – Sweet potato

In Vietnam, white potatoes aren't common. They are replaced by the sweet potato, which is less crunchy and slightly sweet.

In the South, there are several types of sweet potatoes: *khoai lang trắng,* larger than the others, with a grey skin and starchy texture, is not very sweet. *Khoai lang bí* is longer with a purplish red exterior; inside, the flesh is less starchy and sweeter. Although similar in appearance, *khoai lang mật* (honey) is even better. Its pumpkin-colored flesh is very tender, and secretes a honey-like substance. It is eaten as a treat, barely cooked. This is a specialty of Dalat.

Khoai mì – Cassava

Cassava is very easy to grow: when the soil is fertile you can just stick a piece of cassava stalk in the ground and harvest some tubers a few months later. Beware: the large ones are tough!

Khoai mì bào – Grated cassava

In the past, you had to grate the tuber yourself, but nowadays, frozen grated cassava is readily available.

Khoai môn – Taro

Taro tubers come in a variety of sizes: there are very large ones as well as smaller ones, similar in size to a white potato. They are used principally in desserts and soups.

Khoai tây – White potato

The white potato is not used much in Vietnam; it is replaced by the more common sweet potato.

Lá dứa – Pandan leaf

The pandan leaf, used to add fragrance to numerous desserts, also gives them a characteristic green tint. You can sometimes buy frozen concentrated juice; however, it is never as fragrant as the juice prepared from fresh leaves. You may run across *lá dứa* essence, which can perhaps be used to add color, as to its taste, it is nothing compared to freshly extracted pandan juice.

Lá lốt – Wild betel leaf

This sweetly fragrant leaf is related to the betel nuts that Vietnamese women used to chew. Though cheap in Vietnam, it is pricier elsewhere. It is used for wrapping beef before grilling (you can replace it with grape leaves, but *lá lốt* is a lot tastier). For a faster preparation, you can also chop and sauté it with minced beef.

Lạp xưởng – Chinese sausage

A small dried red sausage, a bit sweet. It's not so simple to make, and those who know how to keep the recipe a secret. The only certainty is that it contains pork fat, pork meat and a large variety of optional ingredients such as alcohol and liver.

Laurel (bay leaf)

As laurel doesn't grow in Vietnam, it is practically unknown there. It turns up only in foreign dishes like curry or stew.

Levure Alsacienne - Baking powder

The French Alsa brand baking powder, in its little pink envelope, is the one that works best in Vietnamese recipes. Pay attention, as some recipes call for a special yeast (*men*).

Mắm lóc – Preserved snakehead fish

Mắm lóc is made with the freshwater *cá lóc,* a fish that resembles pollack or hake. It comes in glass jars, already "cleaned." Although it is not the most prized type of *mắm*, it is a little more expensive than others. It is used for *mắm chưng* and *mắm thái*.

Mắm nêm – Ground preserved anchovies

Rather prized, a bit costlier than the other types of *mắm*, this is made with *cá cơm,* a kind of very small anchovy. It usually comes as a very liquid sauce, sometimes containing small bits of fish and bones. It is the traditional accompaniment for *bò nhúng dấm*. If *mắm nêm* is unavailable, *mắm tôm* or *mắm ruốc* are substituted.

Mắm ruốc – Shrimp paste

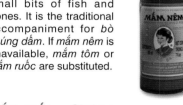

This is a thick paste that should be purplish-pink. Simply accompanied with rice and fresh cucumber, it serves as a makeshift meal. It is a good condiment for the various fondues.

The Southern and Central Vietnamese are more knowledgeable on *mắm* than the Northerners and can differentiate between *mắm tôm,* which is brown, made with small shrimp, and *mắm ruốc,* which is purple and prepared with a different tiny crustacean.

Mắm sặc – Preserved gouramy fish

Mắm sặc is produced with *cá sặc*, a small fish that is normally eaten fried, while setting the smallest ones aside to make *mắm*. This type of *mắm*, sold in glass jars, is really salty!

Mắm thái – Prepared fillet of *mắm lóc*

Fillet of *mắm lóc* is shredded and then seasoned with honey and roasted rice flour (*thính*). When it is served, grated papaya is added. It is eaten with boiled pork belly, cucumber, and herbs.

Mắm tôm – Shrimp paste

Similar to *mắm ruốc*, *mắm tôm* is made with larger shrimp; it is grey-colored and less appetizing. Nevertheless, it has a similar taste, and in fact, in the North, people don't distinguish between *mắm tôm* and *mắm ruốc*. The North Vietnamese always add one or two drops of *cà cuống* in their *mắm tôm*. The slightly pink *mắm tôm* from *Huế* is quite famous.

Măng – Bamboo shoot

There is a huge variety of bamboo shoots, although not all are edible. This vegetable "that is a gift from heaven" is found everywhere in Vietnam, from North to South, and is eaten in many ways: in soups, in salads, sautéed, salted, dried, in brine...

Outside Vietnam, bamboo shoots are mostly sold in cans, already cooked. If you can see the striations on the inside, they will be tender. But watch out: canned

bamboo sometimes has a strong odor and therefore must be rinsed well before using. You can sometimes find fresh shoots (*măng mạnh tông*) in supermarkets. These should not be confused with shoots that have been previously canned and sold in bulk. The fresh shoots are definitely better and have no odor.

Măng tây – Asparagus

Literally "French bamboo," asparagus is not native to Vietnam. An rare item that is grown only in Dalat, it is affordable only for the rich. It is used mainly on special occasions, in crab and asparagus soup.

Me - Tamarind

It is often called "*me chua*" (sour tamarind), which is redundant since tamarind is always sour. Its sweet and sour touch pleasantly enhances the flavor of broths. It is sold dried, but also, and more

practically, in the form of a small loaf, with or without seeds. You need to boil it and filter the resulting juice. When tamarind is not available, you can replace it with vinegar or lemon juice.

Mè - Sesame seed

("*Vừng*" in the North) In very poor families, toasted salted sesame seeds can be eaten with rice as a substitute for meat. However, they have a multitude of other uses: as a garnish for banana cake or for *chè*, in candies (*mè xửng*) and many more. Pay attention when

toasting the seeds as they burn quickly. You need to stir continuously over medium heat so that the inside has time to cook while the outside becomes a nice golden brown without turning black.

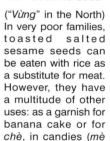

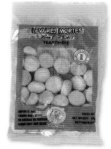

Men cơm rượu – Yeast for rice wine

This special yeast is 100% Vietnamese and will be found in any Asian supermarket that sells Vietnamese products. It is used to prepare *cơm rượu*, a very popular dessert with a rice wine fragrance.

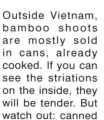

Mì – Wheat noodle

Although they are sometimes translated as "egg noodles," literally "*mì*" means "wheat": these noodles are thus of Chinese origin, as wheat is not cultivated in Vietnam. Nevertheless, sautéed wheat noodles (*mì xào*) are ever present in Vietnam, accompanied by all sorts of garnishes: beef, pork, or seafood. They are usually sold in the shape of nests. You can find them fresh or dried.

Miến – Mung bean thread

Also called "cellophane noodle, glass noodle, mung bean vermicelli, or mung bean noodles," and equally known as "*bún tàu*" in Vietnam, this ingredient is not made with a classic flour, but with mung beans. It is not to be confused with vermicelli or rice noodles: although starchy, *miến* is not in the same category. Mung bean thread are always soaked before using.

Mushroom seasoning

This Chinese vegetable-based condiment has appeared recently and can replace the controversial MSG for intensifying the taste of stocks and soups.

Nấm hương – Shiitake mushroom

One of the most expensive Asian mushrooms, it is sold fresh or dried. Fresh ones are often found under their Japanese name "shiitake." This fragrant mushroom is very widespread in Vietnam, but only in its dried form. If you forgot to soak the mushrooms a long time in advance, you can get by with 1 to 2 hours in very hot water.

Nấm mèo – Wood ear mushroom

Literally "cat mushroom" in Vietnamese, this inexpensive product is always sold dried. As it has little flavor, it serves mostly to add crunchiness and texture to the dishes. A more literary name is "*mộc nhĩ*" meaning "vegetable ears," because it grows on tree trunks and the smaller ones are rather in the shape of an ear.

Nấm rơm – Straw mushroom

When fresh, this cute little round yellow-brown mushroom is crunchy and tasty. Unfortunately, it doesn't travel well: you can find it in cans, but by then it has lost most of its flavor. It is often included in mixed sautéed vegetables.

Nem chua – Small fermented pâté

These small pâtés are made from pounded raw pork (in Vietnam, until the appearance of electric food processors, a mortar and pestle were used). Roasted rice flour is normally added along with saltpeter and spices. They are wrapped in small cubes and left to ferment for several days. The result is a compact meat, which will keep about 10 days.

Nếp – Glutinous or sticky rice

See "*Gạo nếp.*"

Nghệ – Turmeric

Some Vietnamese refer to it (incorrectly) as "saffron," because the two powders are similar in color. Saffron is, in reality, the pistil of a flower, whereas *nghệ* is a rhizome, somewhat similar to ginger though more colorful. Moreover, it is far cheaper than saffron. Its use is reserved for certain dishes, more often fish.

In the South, it is mixed with water and brushed on the bellies, and even the faces of pregnant women to combat stretch marks.

Ngò – Cilantro

Also called "coriander," this aromatic herb looks somewhat like parsley but has a completely different taste and a very distinctive fragrance. In Vietnamese cooking, cilantro is used as a garnish to finish the presentation and is often combined with scallions. It is not normally part of the platter of salad and aromatic herbs.

Ngò gai – Culantro

Also called "saw-leaf" or "saw-tooth" herb. Even though its literal meaning is "prickly cilantro," this herb is, in fact, not related to true cilantro, nor does it look much like it. It is used to season sour soup (*canh chua*), in which it is mandatory. It is also used raw in salads.

Ngò om – Rice paddy herb

This herb with a lemon fragrance does not belong to the cilantro family (*ngò*), in spite of its Vietnamese name. It gets its English name from the fact that it likes to grow in water. It is never eaten raw, but it is used to add flavor in soups such as sour soup or giant taro soup (*canh khoai mỡ*).

Ngó sen – Lotus stem

All over Asia, the lotus has great symbolic significance, but it has a practical value as well: the flower can be eaten as well as the seeds and the stem. The leaves are used to wrap *cốm dẹp*. As it grows in ponds, the people go to harvest it in small tapered boats.

The stems are usually sold in glass jars, sometimes with water, sometimes with vinegar: you will need to take that into account and adjust the final seasoning of the dish.

Nước cốt dừa – Coconut milk

(Also coconut extract, or coconut cream) Coconut palms, uncommon in the North, grow in dense forests all over the South. Coconut is pervasive in the Southern cuisine, to the extent that it is found indifferently in sweet and savory dishes as well as broths. All Southern cakes will contain some coconut, which is not the case

in Central or Northern Vietnam: you can in fact say that desserts using coconut are unknown in the North. Coconut is also made into cooking oil as well as a cosmetic product for hair.

Theoretically, "*nước cốt dừa*" should be a pure coconut extract, obtained by pressing and grating fresh coconut meat (not to be confused with coconut juice for drinking). After the juice is extracted, water is added and the coconut is kneaded and pressed again. It is necessary to let the second press sit and remove the foam that forms before incorporating it into the first press.

In reality, the products sold under the name "*nước cốt dừa*" (coconut milk, coconut cream, or coconut extract) are rather variable: you'll need to read the ingredients to determine their exact composition. The best brands have less water than the inferior ones.

Nước mắm – Fish sauce

If you needed to pick only one ingredient that characterizes Vietnamese cooking, it would have to be *nước mắm*! It is manufactured by collecting the liquid produced from the maceration of fish. The best is prepared with anchovies, but nowadays it is made with all sorts of fish, even shrimp or squid. The Southern people are more knowledgeable about it that those from the North, as the waters in the South have more fish, and anchovies, found there in profusion, produce the best *nước mắm* in the world, often imitated, but never equaled!

The most reputable brand is *Nước Mắm Phú Quốc,* made in Vietnam, but beware of imitations! Although it is produced now in Thailand and the Philippines, true *nước mắm* is 100% Vietnamese. Pay attention to the degree, and prefer 35° over the blander 25°. Good *nước mắm* has a beautiful amber color: once the bottle is opened, it should be refrigerated to prevent darkening.

Nước tro tàu – Lye water

A white liquid, previously obtained from the ashes of a special wood. It has the virtue of making dough crunchier. It has some similarities to baking soda.

Ớt – Chili pepper

In the Southern Vietnamese countryside, chili plantations stretch as far as the eye can see. Although the Vietnamese don't spice up their food as much as the Thais (Central Vietnam excepted), the chili pepper is absolutely indispensable as a condiment. Whenever they can, housewives grow a pot of peppers in their apartments, and children start eating them at a very young age. There are numerous species, from very large to very small (like the fiery hot bird or bird's eye chili pepper).

Phổ tai – Dried seaweed

This is found throughout Asia. The Vietnamese eat it only in *chè*, as opposed to agar-agar, another algae-based product. It is sold either as large leaves or already cut into small pieces. You need to soak and rinse it thoroughly before use.

Rau giấp cá – Fish herb

(Or *rau diếp cá*) This is a medicinal plant known all over Vietnam, North to South: the leaf is crushed to extract a juice that is given to cure fever. A poultice is made from the rest. It also has a reputation for lowering blood pressure.

It is an aromatic herb whose sight and smell will make the South Vietnamese drool. The people in the Center or North, though, are generally in horror of it. Those who appreciate it find that it marvelously complements fish and *nước mắm* in all its forms. However, as its flavor is quite pronounced, it doesn't go with everything.

It can also be eaten in salad with sliced hard-boiled eggs, sprinkled with a bit of *nước mắm* dip.

Rau húng – Mint

Abroad, mint is used frequently, as it is readily available, but in Vietnam, mint is not particularly special and many other aromatic herbs are used as well.

Rau húng quế – Vietnamese basil

This fragrant herb has leaves resembling mint, though less serrated. It differs also in that its stalk is brown and stiffer. In spite of its name, ordinary "Western" basil cannot be used as a substitute: its fragrance is quite different and would clash with the other flavors.

Rau muống – Water spinach

The emblem of the Northerners! This plant with its long hollow stalk and slender leaves was originally a very inexpensive vegetable, growing in any puddle, pond, or stagnant water. Nowadays, *rau muống* has truly become the national vegetable: Vietnamese emigrants are very fond of it, and though it is costly, continue to consume it with pleasure.

In order for the leaves to retain a nice green color, don't forget to salt the boiling water when blanching. The cooking water is very popular in the North; in the South, they throw it out.

Rau om – Rice paddy herb

See "*Ngò om.*"

Rau răm – Polygonum

Also called "Vietnamese cilantro," this peppery aromatic herb holds an important place in Vietnamese cooking: for salads (*gỏi*), traditionally no other herb is used. It is easily recognized by its long pointy leaves. Be careful, it spoils quickly: it's best to wash and dry the leaves as soon as you get home.

You can make soup with it (*canh rau răm*): in a very hot broth, add beef slices and chopped *rau răm*, then season with salt, pepper, and *nước mắm*.

However, like parsley, it has a bad reputation for being abortive.

Rau tần ô – Chrysanthemum leaf

This is the national vegetable of North Vietnam and also called "*cải cúc*" there. It is eaten raw, sautéed, or in soup and is an indispensable ingredient in *lẩu*.

Riềng – Galanga

Or "galangal." Rather similar to ginger, this rhizome is pink-tinted and milder. Though used less commonly than ginger, it is nevertheless indispensable in certain dishes. In general, galanga is paired with fish, while ginger is associated more often with meat.

Sả – Lemongrass

This all-weather plant, also known as "citronella," proliferates in dry or wet conditions and is particularly popular with the middle class. Typically, all families would grow some in their gardens.

The lemongrass fragrance goes well with meat and fish, and even in soups. You can crush an entire stalk then cut it into pieces or chop it finely to release its aroma. Mixed with salt and fresh chili pepper, it serves as a baste before frying fish. It is used with salt and oil to season grilled meat.

Before chopping, be sure to remove the bottom of the stalk and the hard outer leaves.

Sương sa – Agar–agar

Agar-agar, very popular in Vietnam, is consumed in many forms, sweetened or plain. Boiled then cooled, it is used to make jellies. It is available in Asian markets ready to use in the form of strings resembling raffia. In France, agar-agar used to be sold in pharmacies as a laxative!

Agar-agar is often served with mock pomegranate seeds (*hạt lựu*), made by mixing tapioca flour with food coloring (or grenadine syrup) and water. The resulting paste is spread and cut into small seeds, then thrown into boiling water until the outside is translucent, the interior remaining opaque.

The agar-agar jelly is cut into small cubes, then a spoonful of "pomegranate seeds," a bit of grenadine syrup, and a spoonful of coconut milk are added. It should be served very cold. In Vietnam, street vendors often keep the agar-agar in a large plastic basin. In its center is an upside-down bowl and on it, a large piece of ice. As the ice slowly melts, cold water leaks into the dessert and cools it.

Táo tầu – Chinese date or jujube

Literally "Chinese apple." The young fruit resembles a light green plum. At maturity, it becomes dark red and takes the appearance of a small date. It is sold dried, pitted or not, very dry for cooking, less dry if for immediate consumption.

A rather expensive ingredient, best known in *chè bột khoai*, it is not widely used. It is sometimes found in medical preparations.

Tầu hủ – Tofu

Called *tầu hủ* in the South and *đậu phụ* in the North (the "t" being the Chinese pronunciation of the Vietnamese "đ"), tofu, or bean curd, is made from real soy (*đậu nành*) and not mung bean. It is used in many ways, as a vegetable or as a meat substitute: you can fry or sauté it; you can cook it in a double boiler with shrimp paste and season it with sesame oil; you can stuff it with meat or make a soup with ground meat, a cut tomato, and other ingredients... It is truly a national food! It keeps a long time if immersed in water.

Thảo quả – Black cardamom

These very fragrant pods, the size of a small walnut do belong to the cardamom family, though their fragrance and shape are very different from those of the more usual green cardamom. They are sometime erroneously cataloged as "nutmeg." In Vietnam, their main usage is in the stock for *phở*.

Thìa là – Vietnamese dill

Thìa là resembles classic dill, but with a shorter stalk. If available, it is preferred to regular dill, as its aroma is stronger. It is more widespread in the North than in the South and, like everywhere else on the planet, is primarily used with fish.

Thính – Roasted rice flour

In olden days, *thính* was prepared at home by roasting raw rice over low heat until it became golden-brown and released a pleasant aroma. It then was reduced to flour using a mortar. Happily, it can now be found fully prepared in Asian markets.

If you insist on doing it yourself, you will need to grind it a long time in order to get a fine powder.

Tía tô – Perilla

This aromatic herb, with its pretty leaf, green on top and purple on the bottom, is related to the Japanese "shiso." Though it's normally present on the traditional platter of salad and herbs, not everyone appreciates its strong flavor.

It has medicinal uses, for example, as an herbal tea with ginger and honey for sore throats.

Tiêu – Pepper

Pepper grows abundantly in Vietnam. The most prized is that of *Phú Quốc;* however, pepper trees are not a rare sight in the gardens in Saigon. Grey or white, Vietnamese pepper is similar to that found in the West but with coarser and more fragrant peppercorns.

Tỏi – Garlic

Garlic and onion are used very frequently in Vietnamese cooking, and the Vietnamese consume quite a large amount of both.

Tôm - Shrimp

Freshwater and saltwater shrimp are plentiful in South Vietnam. In the North, they are rarer and costlier. Previously, wild shrimp were so abundant in the countryside that people would set out in small boats and gather them at will. However, with intensive organized fishing, they became rarer. Nowadays, thanks to both family and large-scale farming, they have made a comeback and Vietnam has become a shrimp-exporting country.

Shrimp are best if cooked in the shell: plunge them in boiling salt water and pull them out as soon as they are pink and opaque (2 or 3 minutes). However, it is easier to shell and devein them when raw. Shelled shrimp should be steamed instead of boiled to preserve the flavor.

Tôm khô – Dried shrimp

Dried shrimp are typically Asian. If they were very fresh to start with, the final product has a bright pink color. If not, it's dull or gray.

They serve as a snack: soaked in vinegar and sugar, they go well with beer. They also add flavor to stocks. Sometimes, they are used to make a savory broth without meat, simply adding vegetables.

Tương – Fermented beans

These beans come in numerous forms: whole (tương hột), ground, formed into small cubes, or liquid. They are seasoned with chili pepper or other spices. Ground, they serve as a condiment, much in the same way as nước mắm (tương is to North Vietnam what nước mắm is to the South).

Tương hột đen is a Chinese product always sold in cans or jars, made with black beans. The yellow bean, softer and sweeter, is similar. These two products, however, have very different uses: for example, the black bean is used for steamed fish, while the yellow bean enters in the composition of sauces, like peanut sauce. The specifically Vietnamese tương is tương bắc.

Tương bắc – Fermented bean sauce

As its name indicates, this is a product of North Vietnam ("bắc" meaning "north" in Vietnamese). Even though, following the massive migration of "Northerners" in 1954, it has gained some reluctant popularity in the South, tương bắc has stayed the specialty of the North. Traditionally, all the housewives prepare it once a year: in large earthenware jars with a capacity of several dozen liters, they layer soybeans (đậu nành) with sticky rice and a special type of mold. After fermentation, the mahogany-colored liquid at the surface is collected and saved preciously. The bottom of the jar contains tương bắc itself.

It is sold in bottles and is available almost everywhere: the most prized is "tương cự đà," which was the name of a village that produced it, but now all producers call it by that name... This tương, typically Vietnamese, is very popular with water spinach, fried tofu, or other vegetables. It can also be used as a marinade for tiny eggplants (cà pháo).

Tương ngọt – Hoisin sauce

A Chinese condiment based on soybeans, chili peppers, sugar, and salt. In order to save work, people tend to use it to replace peanut sauce, which is too bad. Used sensibly, it is a good condiment.

Vị – Star anise

This spice, ubiquitous in Asia, is in the form of a little eight-pointed star. It has no connection with regular anise, its taste being closer to fennel or licorice.

Xá xíu – Chinese roast pork

All Vietnamese housewives prepare this dish. However it is 100 % Chinese.

Nowadays, we use pork loin or shoulder, seasoned with a special mix sold in Asian markets. You can also buy it ready to eat from Chinese caterers.

Xì dầu – Soy sauce

Even though the soy sauce found in Vietnam is of Chinese origin, its usage is very widespread, almost as much as nước mắm or salt. On the other hand, it was only after the emigration of Chinese out of Vietnam that nước mắm started showing up in some Chinese restaurants.

Xoài - Mango

The Vietnamese mango is, of course, the best! These stand out particularly:

- xoài voi: round and plump, 4 inches long, a light yellow skin, sweet with a fine texture. Unfortunately, this species has disappeared.

- xoài thanh-ca: a bit longer and flatter than the previous one, with dark yellow skin. Its pit is very flat and practically nonexistent; the fruit is as sweet as honey.

- xoài cát: a hybrid species that appeared several decades ago, very large (therefore very profitable) and almost as good as xoài voi. It is now considered the best, since the other two species (xoài voi et xoài thanh-ca) are disappearing.

- xoài tượng: plump like xoài voi, but larger (5 inches long at least). It's eaten when it barely reaches maturity, its fruit becoming a bit yellow, sweet, tangy, and very crunchy. This is exactly the sort of fruit prized by the Vietnamese. It must be shared between 4 or 5 people—it is that big! Street merchants cut it in slices and macerate it in a sweet and salty, anise-scented liquid.

- xoài gòn: is also eaten before maturity, sometime with salt and crushed chili pepper.

There are many other mango species with varied uses. For gỏi, the "Kent" species works well: it is crunchy and tart with a nice consistency. They can be found all year, but choose those that are very hard to the touch.

Index and Glossary

Table of Contents